THE REVEALING STORY BEHIND THE YEAR'S MOST SHOCKING HORROR FILM!

THE BLAIR WITCH PROJECT, an independently produced movie concerning the disappearance of three student filmmakers while researching the legend of the Blair Witch, was the surprise hit of the 1999 Sundance Film Festival, and was the only English-language film to win an award at Cannes. Only by exclusive arrangement with the missing students' families was Haxan Films able to assemble the students' footage (found a full year after their disappearance) into a narrative of their doomsday ride into the Black Hills of Maryland, a journey both mysterious and terrifying in its implications.

The book you hold in your hands takes that journey one step further.

Using official police files, transcripts of recorded interviews, exclusive archive photographs, and the actual case reports prepared for the students' families by private investigator C. D. "Buck" Buchanan, noted occult journalist D. A. Stern unearths the most comprehensive dossier surrounding the disappearance of Heather Donahue, Joshua Leonard and Michael Williams . . .

and the legend of the Blair Witch. . . .

D. A. Stern has been investigating the occult and related phenomena for over twenty years. He has written several previous works including *Witchcraft: Primal Persecution*, and *European Folklore in America*. In addition, he served as executive consultant on the recent television mini-series "The Salem Witch Trials."

THE BLAIR WITCH PROJECT

D. A. Stern

AN ONYX BOOK

ONYX
Published by New American Library, a division of
Penguin Putnam Inc., 375 Hudson Street,
New York, New York 10014, U.S.A.
Penguin Books Ltd, 27 Wrights Lane,
London W8 5TZ, England
Penguin Books Australia Ltd, Ringwood,
Victoria, Australia
Penguin Books Canada Ltd, 10 Alcorn Avenue
Toronto, Ontario, Canada M4V 3B2
Penguin Books (N.Z.) Ltd, 182–190 Wairau Road,
Auckland 10, New Zealand

Penguin Books Ltd, Registered Offices:
Harmondsworth, Middlesex, England

First published by Onyx, an imprint of New American Library, a division of Penguin Putnam Inc.

ISBN: 0-7394-0558-6

Printed in the United States of America
Set in Garamond Light Condensed
Designed by Stanley S. Drate/Folio Graphics Co. Inc.

ACKNOWLEDGMENTS

Thanks to everyone at Penguin Putnam, Haxan, Artisan, and Folio who helped put this book together, most especially: Dan Slater, Rob Cowie, Stan Drate, Katherine Lawton, Gregg Hale, Amorette Jones, Lucas Mansell, Mike Monello, Dan Myrick, Jessica Rovello, Ben Rock, Ed Sanchez, and Kyle Thorpe. Others whose contributions should not go unrecognized include Llewellyn Press, Dunkin' Donuts, Richard Hunt, and Kevin "Bud" Votel. My love and gratitude to Jill, Madeleine, Toni, and Cleo for space on the couch.

Special mention must be made here of Diane Ahlquist and Buck Buchanan, without whose active and enthusiastic cooperation the writing of this book would have been impossible.

Haxan Films would especially like to thank Christian Guevarra, Ethan Long, Julia Fair, and the West Volusia Historical Society.

NOTE FROM THE AUTHOR

When I was eight years old, I made a decision that changed my life.

My memory of the particulars is a bit fuzzy: as I remember it now, it was a hot summer evening, a Saturday night, and I just couldn't fall asleep. So I tiptoed past my parents' bedroom, and snuck downstairs to watch television.

Those of you who grew up in the New York area might remember *Chiller Theater*, a late-night horror film show whose opening credits featured a stark, twisted hand rising up out of the ground. An ominous voice incanted the single word "Chiller" as the hand disappeared back into the muck.

That evening, I turned on the television just in time to see those opening credits and hear the announcer declare, "Tonight's *Chiller Theater* presentation is *Dracula Has Risen From the Grave*."

I almost ran in terror.

In a sense, I've spent the rest of my life trying to recreate that electrifying bone-chilling fear I felt during that show's opening, that moment when dripping blood hits Christopher Lee's lips, and in defiance of all the laws of nature, unholy life pours back into his body, and his eyes flicker open.

In search of that same thrill, I watched every horror film that came on television, pored over every book I could get my hands on, and eventually began to research the origins of the various creatures featured in those stories—the demons, vampires, werewolves and, of course, witches.

Which is where things begin to get really scary.

I discovered some of the old legends have their basis in actual phenomena for which, to this day, the scientific world has no explanation. It was while researching some of those legends for my college senior thesis—specifically, the various religions and "nature cults" that existed in pre-Christian Europe—that I first came across mention of the Blair Witch. In one treatise, a half-dozen American folk tales were mentioned: the Blair Witch was the only one on the list that I was unfamiliar with.

Intrigued, I began to do a little more research into the legend. I had a surprisingly difficult time finding primary source material and, because the Blair Witch wasn't central to my thesis, soon abandoned my efforts.

Twenty years passed.

An anthropologist friend of mine had recently invited me to join her on a dig in Central Europe. Though the expedition failed to turn up the sort of relics I sought, on the flight back to the United States I happened to read an article in *Filmmaker* magazine about a chilling movie called *The Blair Witch Project* that had just been shown at the Sundance Film Festival.

The entire movie consisted of the edited footage that the three Maryland students had shot while attempting to come up with conclusive facts about the Blair Witch themselves—footage that had been found a year after their mysterious disappearance and then assembled by a team of filmmakers at Haxan Films.

When the plane landed in New York, I immediately made contact with Haxan. Fortuitous timing: they had just begun looking for someone to help them organize all of the vast material related to the disappearance of Heather Donahue, Joshua Leonard, and Michael Williams, and a bizarre and notorious backstory they weren't able to fit into their documentary. After a few meetings with Daniel Slater, an editor at Penguin Putnam, the decision was made to proceed with a book that, for the first time, allows the public to catch a terrifying glimpse into The Blair Witch Project.

A brief note: some of the material that follows has been abridged in consideration of relevancy. Buck Buchanan's reports have been reformatted to fit the book's design, and some of these reports appear out of chronological sequence in order to present a more coherent narrative. In the same spirit, notes are included throughout the text where clarification was thought necessary.

D. A. Stern
Las Vegas
May 1999

INTRODUCTION

Three years after student filmmakers Heather Donahue, Michael Williams, and Joshua Leonard disappeared in the forests of Maryland's Black Hills, law-enforcement authorities finally released all of the evidence they had discovered in the case to the students' families. Among the items returned were several reels of black-and-white film and close to a dozen videocassettes that had never before been made public.

Angela Donahue, the most visible and vocal of the parents throughout the entire ordeal, was instrumental in getting all those materials turned over to Haxan Films in their entirety for editing and assembly into what became THE BLAIR WITCH PROJECT.

A few weeks before this book went to press, I had a chance to sit down and talk with the filmmakers at Haxan about the found footage, and how they became involved with the project.

Ed Sanchez (Co-Director): We received a call back in the middle of 1997 from Mike [author's note: Professor Michael DeCoto, at Montgomery College], asking us if we'd be willing to help a friend of his edit some raw footage. He put us in touch with Angela Donahue, and when we found out the whole story from her—well, we were more than a little intrigued.

Gregg Hale (Producer): We were also anxious to get involved with the project.

Dan Myrick (Co-Director): I remember hearing a little bit about the case—I guess it must have been back in '94, when the students first disappeared.

GH: When they asked us to assemble it into a rough cut for all the families, I think they were hoping that the footage was going to provide some answers . . . we were really looking forward to getting all of it because it was going to answer all of our questions. But it really was the opposite.

ES: There are instances in the footage where the three filmmakers run across things they really can't explain—things that are definitely man-made, but you can't really explain them with natural causes.

DM: Absolutely. The other thing is that, as we were reviewing the tapes, we were witnessing this transformation—from this student film about the Blair Witch into a visual diary of the filmmakers. Heather turned the camera on her, Josh, and Mike in an effort—it seems to me—to leave some kind of record.

GH: We spent about three months just looking at all the footage before trying to assemble it. And once we did that—we found that we had more questions than we had before.

Haxan had at their disposal not just the found footage, but a great deal of other information related to the students' disappearance. In January of 1996, at the recommendation of her father-in-law, Randy Donahue, Angela Donahue had hired a Washington, D.C., investigative firm—Buchanan's Private Investigative Agency—to augment the work being done by law enforcement authorities.

The agency's head, C. D. "Buck" Buchanan, Jr., employed a team of several detectives full-time for several months, sparing no effort or expense in the attempt to find some trace of the missing students. For their reference, Angela Donahue supplied Haxan films with every piece of evidence Buck Buchanan and his investigators dug up.

This book contains virtually all of that evidence, as well as additional material recently supplied to the author.

The Haxan Team (from left to right): Dan Myrick, Robin Cowie, Gregg Hale, Michael Monello, Eduardo Sanchez.

PHOTO BY JULIE ANN SMITH.

CONTENTS

OVERVIEW 1

THE FOOTAGE 7

THE SEARCH 35

THE STUDENTS 59

THE BLAIR WITCH 99

RUSTIN PARR 123

HEATHER'S JOURNAL 143

THE BLACK HILLS 171

THE AFTERMATH 183

OVERVIEW

A timeline of the events surrounding the disappearance of Heather Donahue, Joshua Leonard and Michael Williams.

OCTOBER 20, 1994	The three students arrive in Burkittsville and interview locals about the legend of the Blair Witch.
OCTOBER 21, 1994	Students enter the Black Hills Forest surrounding Burkittsville.
OCTOBER 24, 1994	Students fail to return for classes.
OCTOBER 25, 1994	Police issue an A.P.B. Joshua Leonard's car is soon discovered parked on Black Rock Road.
OCTOBER 26, 1994	Maryland State Police launch an extensive manhunt of the Black Hills area. The search lasts ten days and consumes 33,000 man-hours.
NOVEMBER 5, 1994	The search is called off.
JUNE 19, 1995	Case is classified as "inactive" and left unsolved.
OCTOBER 16, 1995	A backpack full of film equipment and supplies is discovered in the Black Hills Forest. Sheriff Ron Cravens confirms the bag is the property of Heather Donahue and her crew.
DECEMBER 15, 1995	The filmmakers' families are allowed to view sections of the footage.
JANUARY 15, 1996	Frustrated with the official lack of progress on the case, Heather Donahue's family hires private investigator Buck Buchanan.
FEBRUARY 16, 1996	A second group of clips is released. Sheriff Ron Cravens raises the possibility that some of the footage may be faked.
MAY 20, 1996	Final case report submitted by investigator Buchanan to the family of Heather Donahue.
MARCH 1, 1997	The case is once again declared inactive, and remains unsolved.

Buck Buchanan's intensive investigation into the disappearance of Heather Donahue, Joshua Leonard, and Michael Williams lasted several months. His work on the case was not continuous, however, and can be broken down into distinct phases. Accordingly, we have grouped his reports and associated materials together into seven separate sections that echo the course of his inquiry.

Following, the cover letter that accompanied Buchanan's final report to Angie Donahue on May 20, 1996.

BUCHANAN'S
PRIVATE INVESTIGATIVE AGENCY, INC.
Serving Since 1940

FINAL DRAFT

This Report Constitutes
Confidential Work Product and May Further Constitute
Work Product of the Nature of an Attorney-Client Privilege

May 20, 1996
BPIA #: 94-117

To: Angie Donahue
From: C. D. Buchanan
Re: Missing Persons Investigation
Subjects: Heather Donahue, Joshua Leonard, Michael Williams

SYNOPSIS:

This report details the investigation and circumstances surrounding the disappearance of Heather Donahue, Joshua Leonard, and Michael Williams on or about October 21, 1994. Materials provided herein include documents from Burkittsville law enforcement officials, transcripts of interviews conducted by this investigator and his associates, photographs of evidence, persons, and locations associated with the missing students, and expert analysis of the footage taken by the students at the time of their disappearance and rediscovered approximately one year later.

In addition to this investigator, the following personnel worked on this case:

Jennifer Colton
Carlos Sonenberg
Stephen Whately
Diane Ahlquist

All are identified by their respective initials within these reports.

Respectfully submitted,

C. D. Buchanan

Professional Services Center • 2130 Topanga Creek Boulevard • Cummington, VA • 22769-8990
Office: (927) [redacted] • Local Pager: (927) [redacted]

THE FOOTAGE

The first few pages of Buck Buchanan's initial report to Angela Donahue. Note Sheriff Cravens' initial cooperation: Buck later told me that what he didn't put in his report was the phone call he made to a longtime friend of his, Maryland State Senator Carolyn McComas. McComas made a call of her own to Burkittsville Selectman John Davis, who phoned Cravens and requested the Sheriff afford Buck all possible assistance.

Buck's connections weren't enough to help him stay in Cravens' good graces once the sheriff stubbornly decided the students had faked the recently discovered footage.

C. D. "Buck" Buchanan, Jr. Buck has been involved in full-time enforcement/investigative service for thirty-two years. He graduated from the FBI National Academy in 1980.

BUCHANAN'S
PRIVATE INVESTIGATIVE AGENCY, INC.
Serving Since 1940

This Report Constitutes Confidential Work Product and May Further Constitute Work Product of the Nature of an Attorney-Client Privilege

February 12, 1996
BPIA #: 94-117

INVESTIGATIVE SUMMARY TO DATE

January 15, 1996:
After initial contact with Angela Donahue, Investigator Buchanan was engaged to look into the disappearance of Heather Donahue, Joshua Leonard, and Michael Williams. A phone call was placed to Burkittsville Sheriff Ron Cravens, who agreed to a meeting the following morning. Investigator Buchanan engaged the services of three additional private detectives to assist in the investigation.

January 16, 1996

1. Meeting with Sheriff Ron Cravens. Investigator Buchanan expressed his client's frustration over the lack of progress on the case. Sheriff Cravens and Investigator Buchanan agreed to full disclosure of information in the course of continuing investigations to avoid duplication of efforts.
2. Investigator Buchanan was allowed to view portions of found footage not originally released to the filmmakers' families. Some of this footage was highly graphic in nature. No pertinent leads or information was gleaned from this viewing.
3. Investigator Buchanan was allowed access to the complete police files and related evidence of the original search for the students in October/November 1994.

January 17, 1996

1. Investigator Buchanan continued his review of police files and evidence relating to the case.
2. Meeting with Angela Donahue. Investigator Buchanan recommended a course of action, which was agreed upon.

January 18, 1996

1. Investigators Whately and Colton conducted interviews with the professor and students who discovered the filmmakers' footage. Transcripts are included herein.
2. Investigator Buchanan was permitted to send samples of evidence to Checkmark Consulting, an independent testing laboratory, for chemical analysis.
3. Investigator Sonenberg visited the site where the footage was discovered.
4. Investigator Sonenberg visited the county courthouse and obtained documentation relating

to the evidence site. On review of this documentation, it was decided that further investigation relating to the evidence site would be unproductive.

January 19, 1996

1. Investigator Buchanan engaged the services of another private investigator, retired FBI agent Frank Lauriat, to analyze the footage and associated evidence. A summary of his findings is included herein.

2. Investigator Whately consulted with Sheriff Cravens and Deputy Hart of Burkittsville regarding their interviews with Montgomery College faculty and students. After discussion with Investigator Buchanan, it was decided that further interviews would be conducted.

January 22, 1996

1. With the permission of Sheriff Ron Cravens, Investigator Buchanan sent a copy of the footage to Investigator Lauriat for further analysis.

2. Investigators Colton and Whately began interviewing Montgomery College professors and students, as well as friends of the missing persons. Transcripts provided.

January 23-25, 1996

1. Investigators Colton and Whately completed interviews at Montgomery College. Transcripts provided. No additional information of consequence was discovered.

2. Investigator Buchanan began interviews with family members of the missing students.

January 26-29, 1996

Investigator Buchanan completed interviews with family members. No additional information of consequence was discovered.

January 30, 1996

Investigator Buchanan received from Investigator Lauriat a detailed analysis of the film footage. The analysis noted several anomalies within the footage: a copy of the report is included.

February 2, 1996

1. Investigator Buchanan received the completed laboratory analysis originally requested from Checkmark Consulting on January 18, 1996. A copy of the report is included.

2. Investigator Buchanan consulted with Angela Donahue regarding the results of the completed analyses. They then met with Sheriff Cravens to inform him of the findings of Investigator Lauriat and Checkmark Consulting. Sheriff Cravens requested a meeting with Investigator Buchanan.

February 8, 1996

Meeting with Sheriff Cravens. He informed Investigator Buchanan he believed the footage to be a hoax.

From the Frederick Post, October 19, 1995:

Evidence found in case of missing students

by RODMAN JENKINS
Staff Writer

BURKITTSVILLE -- The first hard evidence in the disappearance of three Montgomery College film students was unearthed earlier this week at an anthropological dig in the Black Hills Forest. The missing students -- Heather Donahue, Joshua Leonard, and Michael Williams -- vanished over a year ago during a weekend trip into the forest to film Ms. Donahue's senior thesis project.

Sheriff Ron Cravens of Burkittsville announced the discovery yesterday in a statement to the press. The evidence, consisting of a backpack filled with audio-visual equipment and several reels of film, was unearthed by students from the University of Maryland during a field dig being supervised by David Mercer, professor of anthropology at the University.

The Sheriff further announced that FBI officials have decided to reopen the case, which consumed over thirty thousand man hours and involved federal and state law enforcement officials before being officially closed in June.

Reached by telephone yesterday evening, Heather Donahue's mother Angela praised the decision to reopen the case. "I've lived without knowing what happened to my daughter for too long. This new evidence will give the police something new to focus their investigation on."

Professor Mercer noted that there was something puzzling about the backpack's discovery. "The pilings for the house have been in the ground since before the Civil War," he stated. "But the backpack was actually found inside the foundation. This, frankly, is more than a bit puzzling since (see EVIDENCE, page A16)

Sheriff Ron Cravens

Below, Sheriff Cravens' press release announcing the discovery of the footage.

BURKITTSVILLE SHERIFF'S OFFICE

Ronald Cravens, Sheriff

October 18, 1995
FOR IMMEDIATE RELEASE

The Burkittsville Sheriff's Office has learned that a backpack which was handed in to this office earlier this week was originally the property of Montgomery College students Heather Donahue, Joshua Leonard, and Michael Williams. The three students, formally declared missing on October 24, 1994, were last seen by two fishermen on the morning of October 21, 1994 as they hiked into the Black Hills Forest just outside Burkittsville.

The backpack was turned in to this office by University of Maryland Professor David Mercer on the afternoon of October 16. Mercer, an anthropology instructor, was supervising a group of students on a field dig when the backpack was discovered. The backpack contained several rolls of exposed film, numerous audio and video cassette tapes, and associated camera equipment. Suspecting a connection to the missing students, one of the videocassettes was viewed, at which point tentative identification of the persons on the film was made by this office. Positive ID was made yesterday evening by the students' families.

The original search for the students was a joint operation conducted by this office and the Maryland State Police, under Federal Bureau of Investigation supervision. More than one hundred volunteers joined law enforcement officials in this ten-day operation, which failed to produce any tangible evidence related to the students' disappearance.

Yesterday afternoon, this office made contact with officials at the FBI, who have advised us that in light of this new evidence, the case will officially be reopened.

The FBI will be setting up a temporary press liaison to handle all media requests for access to the new evidence, as well as interviews with law-enforcement personnel. This liaison is expected to be in place by Monday morning, October 23rd. Until that time, briefings will be conducted by this office at 9:00 a.m. weekday mornings.

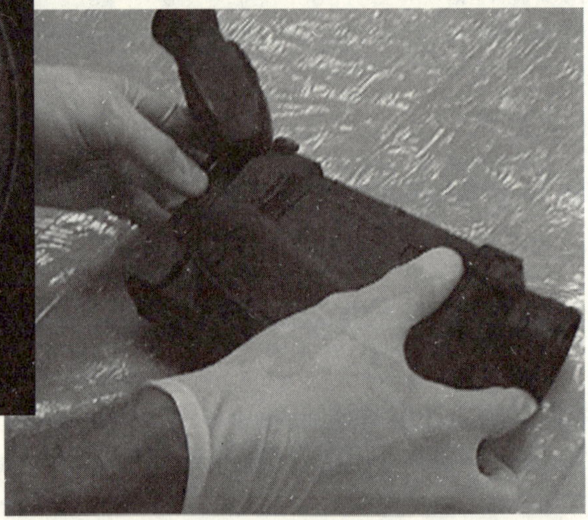

The evidence found in the students' backpack is laid out and catalogued in the Burkittsville Sheriff's Office. The evidence included 16mm film cans, DAT cassettes, a Hi-8, and a CP-16 camera, as well as a journal kept by Heather during their shoot.

From the files of the Burkittsville Sheriff's Office, a copy of the two affidavits signed by Professor Michael DeCoto and Greg Williams that conclusively identified the footage and the students within it. Also, a photograph taken of the backpack just hours after it was found by Professor David Mercer's anthropology class.

BURKITTSVILLE SHERIFF'S OFFICE

Affidavit Of Testimony

Name: GREG WILLIAMS

Address: 57 FOREST GLEN DRIVE, BETHESDA, MARYLAND 20912

Re: Case #: MP01 Date: 10/18/95 Time: 09:45 Officer: HART

I hereby acknowledge and swear that my son, Michael Williams, is one of the persons in the footage shown to me by Sheriff Ron Cravens this afternoon.

Please continue on the back of this form, if necessary.

I Solemnly swear (or affirm) that the statement given above represents the truth as I know it, and hereby acknowledge and understand that I may be liable for prosecution should I present false testimony in regards to a criminal matter.

So Affirmed: Greg Williams

Date: 10/18/95

BURKITTSVILLE SHERIFF'S OFFICE

Affidavit Of Testimony

Name: Michael DeCoto

Address: 344 Dunham place, Rockville MD 20850

Re: Case #: MP01 Date: 10/18/95 Time: 12:27 Officer: HART

I have examined the equipment shown to me by Deputies Hart and Gooding of the Burkittsville Sheriff's department, labeled items and do hereby attest that this material is the property of Montgomery Community College and was originally lent to Heather Donahue for work on her senior thesis project in October of 1994.

I further attest that persons depicted in this footage are known to me as Heather Donahue and Joshua Leonard.

Please continue on the back of this form, if necessary.

I Solemnly swear (or affirm) that the statement given above represents the truth as I know it, and hereby acknowledge and understand that I may be liable for prosecution should I present false testimony in regards to a criminal matter.

So Affirmed: Michael DeCoto

Date: 10/18/

Investigator Jennifer Colton conducts a press briefing for local and national media. A former member of the Baltimore police department, Colton began working for Buck Buchanan in August 1995.

Investigator Stephen Whately. A former New York City police officer, currently working as an investigator for hire to the top agencies in both the U.S. and abroad, Whately received the NYC Departmental Medal of Valor on three separate occasions.

Members of Professor Mercer's anthropology class celebrate the end of a particularly grueling exam week. Peter Gould is at the far right. Andrea Kay Lynn is second from left.

Professor David Mercer.

Extracts from interviews with University of Maryland students and professor who discovered the students' footage. JC is Investigator Jen Colton: SW is Investigator Stephen Whately.

BUCHANAN'S
PRIVATE INVESTIGATIVE AGENCY, INC.

This Report Constitutes Confidential Work Product and May Further Constitute Work Product of the Nature of an Attorney-Client Privilege

January 26, 1996
Re: BPIA #94-117
Transcripts of interviews conducted 1/18/96 (continued)

Peter Gould: That one rock was in there pretty good. When I pulled it out—boom! The whole back half of the basement wall collapsed.

Jen Colton: And that's when you found the backpack?

PG: That's right.

JC: Was there any indication that the ground around the backpack had been disturbed recently?

PG: You mean, like somebody else had been digging there? To bury it?

JC: That's what I mean.

PG: No. Maybe I'm not making myself clear. The wall was intact, the ground was undisturbed, and—

JC: I understand your point—the backpack couldn't have gotten where it was. But it did.

PG: Yes.

JC: Who chose the site of the dig?

PG: Professor Mercer.

JC: Did he choose where—specifically—you would dig on the sixteenth?

PG: That's the day we found the backpack?

JC: Yes.

PG: It's not like we were all standing around, looking for something to do. We had specific sites around the house we were supposed to explore.

JC: Who was digging with you that day?

PG: Let's see—there was me, Andrea, and Tony. And Scott.

JC: That would be Andrea Lynn, Tony Flore, and Scott Darlington.

PG: Uh-huh.

JC: Okay. Thank you, Peter.

This Report Constitutes
Confidential Work Product and May Further Constitute
Work Product of the Nature of an Attorney-Client Privilege

January 26, 1996
Re: BPIA #94-117
Transcripts of interviews conducted 1/19/96 (continued)

Jen Colton: For the record, can you state your name?

Andrea Lynn: Andrea Kay Lynn.

JC: And you're a student at the University of Maryland?

AL: Yes.

JC: And from your transcript, I see that you were previously a student at Montgomery College.

AL: That's right. But I didn't like it, so I dropped out for a couple years and went abroad.

JC: Did you personally know any of the missing students—Heather Donahue, Joshua Leonard, or Michael Williams—while you were at Montgomery?

AL: No, I did not.

JC: On October 16 of last year, you were digging with Professor David Mercer's anthropology class when the footage was recovered.

AL: Yes. Me and Peter—Peter Gould—were actually the ones to find the backpack.

JC: Do you recall anything unusual about the spot you were digging?

AL: No. What do you mean, unusual?

JC: Anything out of the ordinary? Evidence that people had been there recently, for instance.

AL: No. The house is pretty far out in the woods.

JC : How long had the dig been planned?

AL: Well, it was part of the course curriculum.

JC: The actual site?

AL: Well, no, but the fact that we would be going off-campus to dig.

JC: When did you find out where the actual site would be?

AL: Let's see. I guess, not really until a little bit before we left—like, a week or two before. Hah! I get you. You want to find out who knew we were going to be out there, to plant the footage so we could find it.

JC: That's one of the things I want to know, yes. Now, did you all arrive at the dig together that morning?

AL: A bunch of us camped out in the woods the night before. The rest came up with Professor Mercer that morning.

This Report Constitutes
Confidential Work Product and May Further Constitute
Work Product of the Nature of an Attorney-Client Privilege

January 26, 1996
Re: BPIA #94-117
Transcripts of interviews conducted 1/19/96 (continued)

David Mercer: My original intention was that we would study some of the construction techniques and materials used at the time. But a week into the dig, we found some evidence indicating the cabin was used as a way station on the Underground Railroad during the Civil War.

Stephen Whately: What kind of evidence?

DM: A short stretch of hidden passageway—about four feet long—in the basement of the house. It must have gone all the way down to the creek at one point.

SW: That's Tappy East Creek?

DM: Yes. The Creek feeds down into the Potomac. Bill Barnes over at the Historical Society told me a bunch of stories concerning the movement of a great number of slave children and their mothers through this area.

SW: That sounds like a pretty important discovery.

DM: Well, it's definitely something we want to follow up on. But the Sheriff shut us down once we found the footage.

SW: So who first chose this house as the site for your dig?

DM: I did.

SW: Why?

DM: I was out hiking with my family last summer in the woods, and just stumbled onto it.

SW: Okay. Let me back up a second. How many of you were on the dig?

DM: Twelve. Myself and eleven students. All juniors, except for one—Peter. He's a senior.

SW: He's the one who found the footage.

DM: That's correct.

SW: Who told him where to dig that morning?

DM: Peter and a few of the other students had spent the evening camping out in the woods, while the rest of us had gone to a motel in Burkittsville to spend the night. When we got there the next morning, he was already digging.

SW: How did he decide where to dig?

DM: It's fairly standard procedure to dig along the foundation line, as he was doing.

SW: Did you happen to observe him while he was digging?

DM: Well, as I said, his group was already at work when I got there. And Peter was very capable—I'm sorry, I didn't answer your question. No, I didn't watch him dig very long at all.

SW: So you couldn't say whether or not there was anything unusual about the site?

DM: No.

SW: Whether or not it looked to you like someone might have planted the footage?

DM: Well—you understood what I was saying before, about the collapsed wall the backpack was found inside? That's at least one hundred fifty years old. Somebody must have gone to a great deal of trouble to reconstruct it, to put the bag back there.

SW: So you think this is a hoax?

DM: If it is, it's a damn good one.

Professional Services Center • 2130 Topanga Creek Boulevard • Cummington, VA • 22769-8990
Office: (927) ████ • Local Pager: (927) ████

The local press first breaks the news—an article from the November 13th *Frederick Post*.

Students footage suggests foul play

By LELIA WHICKHAM-KELLY
Staff Reporter

BURKITTSVILLE -- Film found near the Black Hills Forest last month suggests that three missing Montgomery College Students may have been stalked by a person/persons unknown before their disappearance.

Sources within the joint task force office set up by the FBI and local authorities confirm that the found footage contains evidence suggesting that Heather Donahue, Joshua Leonard, and Michael Williams met with harm while filming their senior class project in October 1994. Marilyn Slade, spokesman for the joint task force, denied they had reached any conclusions.

"We're still actively working to develop leads based on the information contained in this film," Slade said. "There's a lot of new information here, and it's going to take a while to sort it all out."

The Burkittsville Sheriff's Office organized search efforts by dividing volunteers and law-enforcement officials into separate teams that combed the Black Hills Forest for ten days.

Investigator Carlos Sonenberg. An expert at data processing systems, whose ten-year background in law enforcement includes two years as Chief Deputy for the FBI's Special Archives section.

BUCHANAN'S

PRIVATE INVESTIGATIVE AGENCY, INC.

Serving Since 1940

This Report Constitutes Confidential Work Product and May Further Constitute Work Product of the Nature of an Attorney-Client Privilege

January 22, 1996
BPIA #: 94-117

To: Buck Buchanan

From: Carlos Sonenberg

Re: New Evidence in Missing Persons Case

SYNOPSIS:

Herein, a summary of this investigator's efforts to obtain information regarding the history of the property where on October 16, 1995, objects belonging to missing persons Heather Donahue, Joshua Leonard, and Michael Williams were discovered. Steps taken included physical surveillance of the site, interviews and record searches at the Frederick County Courthouse, as well as research at several local and university libraries.

INVESTIGATIVE DETAILS

January 18, 1996

1. After receiving instructions from Investigator Buchanan, this investigator proceeded to the evidence site, where he was met by Burkittsville Deputy Hank Hart. Because of recent snowfall, the site was difficult to explore thoroughly. Nonetheless, in the opinion of this investigator and Deputy Hart, no additional information beyond that already extensively documented in photographs is to be found at this site.

2. A visit was made to the Park Ranger's office. Ranger Alvin Hunt stated that the house is located in an area of the woods that, although not mapped by the Ranger's office, is directly off a main trail. There are hundreds of visitors to the park each month in the spring and summer. The only recorded visitors to that area in October 1995 were students from Professor David Mercer's anthropology class at the University of Maryland.

3. Frederick County Courthouse was visited, and property records for this area consulted. The house itself appears to have been built shortly after the incorporation of Burkittsville in 1824. The property's earliest recorded owner was a woman named Elizabeth Richardson, who deeded the property to the state shortly before dying. Records for the years since that date are incomplete. Documentation attached.

Professional Services Center • 2130 Topanga Creek Boulevard • Cummington, VA • 22769-8990

Office: (927) ████ • Local Pager: (927) ████

A transcription of one of the property records pulled by Investigator Sonenberg from the Frederick County Courthouse.

To all People to whom these Presents shall come Greeting.

Know ye that I Leslie Stanton of the township of Blair in the Commonwealth of Maryland Yeoman for considerations I swear herein have already been rendered me by Elizabeth Richardson of Blair in the township and State aforesaid have given granted bargained sold and conveyed and confirmed unto the said Elizabeth Richardson one Third Part of one certain Lot of Land lying in Blair in the County and State aforesaid said Lot being the one called Rakone Lot with all the priviledges and appurtenances thereunto belonging to have and to hold the above granted and bargained premises together with all the appurtenances free from all Incumbrances whatsoever to him the said Elizabeth Richardson to her Heirs and Assigns as an absolute Estate of Inheritance in Fee Simple forever and I the said Leslie Stanton do for myself my Heir Executors and Administrators do covenant and engage the above demised Premises to her the said Elizabeth Richardson her Heirs and Assigns against all the lawful claims of any person or Persons whatsoever forever hereafter to warrant and secure and defend by these Presents, in witness hereunto I have set my Hand and seal this third day of January Anno Domini Eighteen hundred and twenty-four.

Signed Sealed and Delivered
in Presents of—

Jeremiah Rider Leslie Stanton of Blair

Nahum Eager

A portion of the lab report prepared for Buck Buchanan. The soil in question is that taken by Investigator Sonenberg on January 18, 1996 from the site where the footage was found. Note the presence of unrefined opiates within the analysis. Opiates and the opium poppy are today associated primarily with heroin usage. Its discovery in the soil here prompted an extensive background check into the missing students' associates, as partially detailed on pages 65–93.

In Paleolithic and Neolithic times, opium was extensively used by those engaged in the practice of witchcraft, both for its psychotropic and narcotic effects.

Checkmark Laboratories
"Industry Leaders since 1949"
2160 Newmarket Parkway
Washington DC 20012

SOURCE INFORMATION:
Buchanan Associates
2130 Topanga Creek Boulevard
Cummington, VA 22769-8990
Contact:
C. D. Buchanan
(927) [redacted]

ACCESS INFORMATION:
F7025831

DATE COLLECTED	DATE RECEIVED	DATE REPORTED
1/18/96	1/25/96	2/1/96

SUMMARY OF SOIL SAMPLE ANALYSIS

Acidity and alkalinity are within normal pH levels. Exchangeable potassium (K), magnesium (Mg), calcium (Ca), sodium (Na), and hydrogen (H) tests were also performed, with test results falling within acceptable norms.

At the customer's request, X-ray absorption fine structure spectroscopy (XAFS) was performed on the sample to determine element specificity. The results are listed in the Appendix in table 2. XAFS revealed an unusually high level of nitrogen compounds (line 25), as well as the presence of minute traces of inspissated opiates (line 26). Other elements were present in expected quantity and percentages—see table for detail.

Given the geographic source of the soil, a testing pattern indicative of clay loam was expected. However, the results herein are reflective of soil more commonly characterized as humus loam, with a higher percentage of decomposed vegetable and animal material than normal. Significant quantities of ash are also present.

Frank Lauriat began his FBI career in 1966, and was a key figure in establishing the agency's Profiling Division in the 1970s. He is trained in both the fields of psychology and law enforcement. He retired from the FBI in 1989, and now works out of his own Washington-based agency.

The following are excerpts from the report Lauriat provided Buchanan on January 20, 1996. Lauriat's text refers to interviews taken by the Burkittsville Sheriff's Office during their initial investigation. These transcripts have been sealed at the families' request.

LAURIAT'S INVESTIGATIVE

P.O. Box 473 • Washington DC 20044 • 1-972-[redacted]

January 20, 1996
Re: BPIA # 94-117

. . . all three show the effects of marked sleep deprivation, exposure, and malnourishment. As requested, a brief rundown on each student follows.

Heather Donahue: Footage corroborates the impression given by the police interview material you showed me. Heather is a stable, level-headed, determined young woman. Until the day the Leonard boy disappears from their tent.

Her sudden psychological collapse at that particular moment is indicative of a chemical imbalance. Drug abuse is one possibility: though more likely it's something genetic, a history of depression or mental illness within her family that could have been triggered by diet or stress. With that in mind, I'd take another look at those journal entries you mentioned. Look for a correspondence between her written lucidity, her behavior as seen in the footage, and an external factor.

Joshua Leonard: A prototypical example of a "troubled" youth. Unfortunately, as the interviews make all too clear, the parents were completely unaware of their son's problems; a sad case. There's nothing in the footage to contradict what police and school officials said about him: he is a classic underachiever. The point in the footage where he simply "shuts off" is telling.

If you're going to look into the three kids' backgrounds for associates who might have been involved in their disappearance, he's the one to focus on.

Michael Williams: Very much a follower—psychologically speaking, he had little choice in the matter. Look again at the transcript where Sheriff Cravens interviews the boy's father—or should I say, where the father interviews Sheriff Cravens. You can tell Michael never was given the opportunity to make a single choice in his life. Resentment at those boundaries, no doubt, will shape the rest of his days. It's that resentment that explodes when he destroys the map: there's no evil intent there.

Summary:

I have to conclude that there's little I can offer you in terms of insight. The footage is too confusing, and there's too little of it. What these students were doing in the woods, in my opinion, has nothing to do with what happened to them—though there is one further possibility I need to mention.

The conflicts between the students at times border on the physical. I'd be remiss in not suggesting that whatever happened to them could have been self-inflicted. Assuming you do get the Sheriff to release the rest of the footage to Mrs. Donahue, I'd keep an eye out for that dynamic in particular.

Only after repeated urging from both this reporter and Buck Buchanan did Lauriat agree to let the following note appear in this book. Some personal details have been deliberately obscured, at Lauriat's request.

From the desk of . . .

FRANK LAURIAT

Buck—

Always good to see you—country living clearly agrees with your system. ████ wants us to try too. I tell her that she'll get me out of Washington when Imperial Dragon delivers outside the city limits.

I got an email back from Ray. He'll take a look at that footage if you can get a copy of it up to him. His schedule's pretty light next week, so that's the time to do it, if you can. Truthfully, I don't see the point. There's no doubt in my mind something horrible has happened to those kids. You don't need to be an expert in psychology to see that they were all scared to death—especially that girl.

If I were in your shoes, Buck, I'd walk right over to that girl's mother and tell her to call off the investigation. As far as I'm concerned, she's better off not knowing the details.

I'll call Monday.

Frank

U.S. Geological Map of the Black Hills Forest on next page: true North is toward the top of the map. The expert who prepared this report for Buck Buchanan requested anonymity: the hand-drawn map referred to has since been lost.

Buck—

Sorry it took so long to get this to you—

It's pretty easy to map the locations in the footage to a standard U.S. Geologic Map. I've included a copy of the one that's the most relevant: for the most part, the kids are wandering around in the upper left-hand quadrant of the map. If you look at the hand-drawn "zoomed-in" version I've provided, you can see how the kids got so lost, so quickly. The old trails in there loop around on each other, and the terrain around the hills I've marked "A" and "B" is identical. That's also why they kept going in circles, too.

But there's something strange about the last few minutes of the film—where the two kids go to the house.

Take a look at that part of the footage yourself. You can see they're going up a fairly steep hill. Close to a 45° angle, up at least two hundred feet, altogether.

Problem is, there is no hill like that in the Black Hills area. Nothing with a deviation from ground level of that significance, anyway.

I suppose they could have hiked out of that part of the forest, that we could be seeing them in a different area of the woods. From what you told me, we don't know how much time elapsed between different segments of the footage. It's always possible that the Federal maps of the area are wrong, too.

Setting aside those last five minutes or so, the kids are clearly in the Black Hills. It's hard to believe that none of the search parties were able to find any trace of them.

I've marked my map with some specific locations that would be worth taking a look at if you go into the Hills yourself.

Let me know if there's anything else I can do.

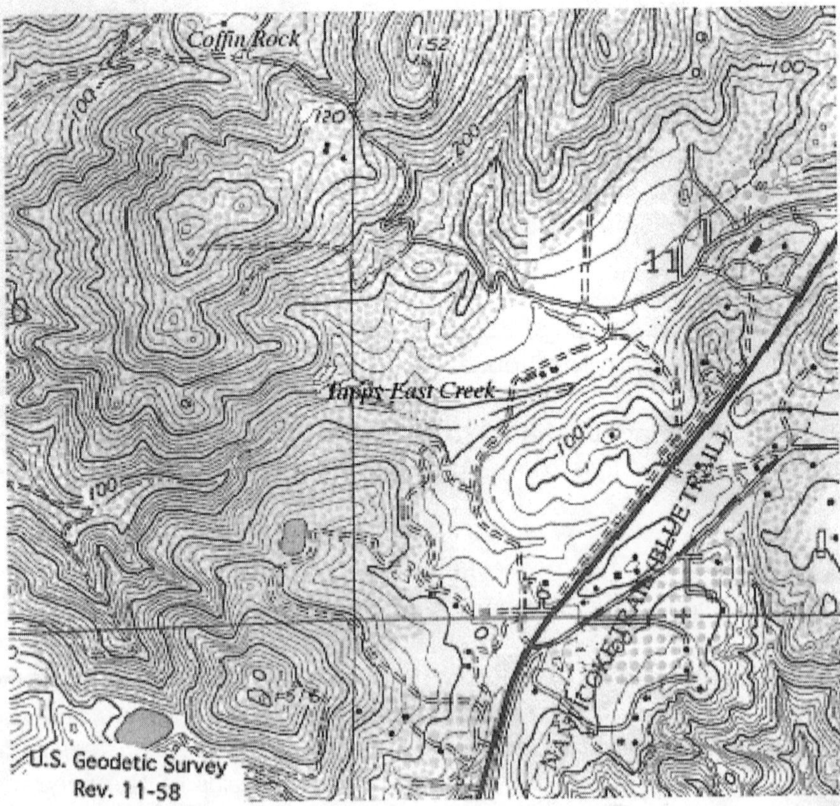

Below and on next page: a falling-out occurs between Sheriff Cravens and the missing students' families. Newspaper articles show the developing rift, which was solidified by Angela Donahue's lawsuit against Cravens. A copy of Judge Dykstra's order of judgment in favor of Burkittsville authorities for return of the evidence uncovered in October 1995 follows. Note Dykstra's reference to the Sheriff having provided "good cause" to retain custody of the evidence.

Task force dissolved

by RODMAN JENKINS
Staff Reporter

Burkittsville -- For the second time in as many years, law enforcement authorities seem to be giving up on Heather Donahue, Joshua Leonard, and Michael Williams.

FBI Spokeswoman Marilyn Slade announced today that senior bureau officials in Washington had decided to disband the joint Federal/State/Local task force currently headquartered in Frederick. The task force was formed in October of this year, after the discovery of film footage apparently shot by the three missing Montgomery College students the weekend they disappeared.

The new evidence apparently failed to generate any significant leads, according to sources within the task force. Nonetheless, those same sources stated, the FBI agents assigned to the case were disappointed in the decision to abandon the inquiry. "It's not special division's style to leave any stone unturned," the source stated. "They like the difficult cases because they have a reputation of solving them. This won't do that reputation any good."

Burkittsville Sheriff Ron Cravens vowed to press forward with the investigation. "I'll admit the footage hasn't given us a lot of new angles to look at, but there are a few things I want to explore. And we don't need a lot of outside help to do that."

Found Footage is Hoax, Cravens Declares

by RODMAN JENKINS
Staff Reporter

BURKITTSVILLE-- Breaking a month-long media silence, Sheriff Ron Cravens spoke directly to representatives of local and national press yesterday, saying that he had reluctantly come to the conclusion that the footage unearthed last October by University of Maryland anthropology students was a hoax.

Authorities originally believed that footage to be a visual record documenting what happened to three Montgomery college students -- Heather Donahue, Joshua Leonard, and Michael Williams -- on an ill-fated trip into the Black Hills Forest. But the footage, according to Sheriff Cravens, contains "numerous inconsistencies" which make it clear that the three students intended it, and its subsequent discovery, as part of a hoax. He declined to elaborate on those inconsistencies, or a possible motive for the students' behavior.

Sheriff Cravens also expressed sympathy for the parents of the missing students, adding that "whatever caused [the students] to pull this kind of stunt, it in no way lessens the anxiety that we all feel over their fate." In light of the new evidence, Sheriff Cravens further announced, he was temporarily suspending further work on the investigation. "There's other business we have to tend to here, but finding these kids remains high on our priority list."

Angela Donahue and Greg Williams, parents of missing students Heather Donahue and Michael Williams, immediately denounced the Sheriff's action. "They're hoping we'll let them sweep this thing under the rug without making a sound, and that ain't gonna happen," declared Williams. Donahue added "It's ridiculous to even suggest my daughter's senior film thesis, which she'd planned and researched for months, was part of some elaborate deception." Donahue added that she'd hired a private investigator at the beginning of the year "whose work on the case will continue."

Heather Donahue, Joshua Leonard, and Michael Williams disappeared almost exactly one year ago (continued on page A21)

LAW OFFICES OF KENNETH W. REED
P.O. Box 366
Hagerstown, MD 27602
Tel: (301)
Fax: (301)
Attorney for Plaintiff

Plaintiff:
ANGELA DONAHUE

SUPERIOR COURT OF MARYLAND

vs

LAW DIVISION:

FREDERICK COUNTY DOCKET NO. 641-422

Defendant:
SHERIFF'S OFFICE
TOWN OF BURKITTSVILLE, and
SHERIFF RONALD CRAVENS

ORDER OF JUDGMENT

This matter coming before the Court by Law Offices of Kenneth W. Reed (Kenneth W. Reed, Esq., appearing), attorney for plaintiff, and defendent having been served with a copy of the summons and complaint, and for good cause:

IT IS ON THIS 2nd day of March, 1996,

ORDERED as follows:

1. Judgment is hereby entered in favor of the defendant, and against plaintiff.

2. Plaintiff is ordered to pay costs of suit.

3. The evidence in question is to remain on the premises of the Burkittsville Sheriff's Office. Moreover, the defendant having provided good cause to retain custody of said evidence, the plaintiff is herein warned against further libelous remarks.

Dykstra J.S.C.

BUCHANAN'S
PRIVATE INVESTIGATIVE AGENCY, INC.
Serving Since 1940

This Report Constitutes Confidential Work Product and May Further Constitute Work Product of the Nature of an Attorney-Client Privilege

February 21, 1996

Angela Donahue

Dear Angela:

I want to thank you again for dinner last night. You and Jim made me feel right at home, and I appreciate that.

Like I told you, don't be too hard on Sheriff Cravens. He's just doing what he thinks is right for him, and his town. That doesn't mean I agree with him: it's just that right now, criticizing him is going to do more harm than good. Go forward with the lawsuit, but please lay off him in the press. And if you can get Greg and Tom Williams to do the same, that would be wonderful.

As for me, I'll repeat what I said at dinner: I do not believe that footage is fake. Since I don't believe in ghosts, or witches, or what-have-you, I have to believe that somebody has done something to cause your daughter and these other young adults to come up missing. I don't know who, I don't know why, but I believe we can find out, that there are still productive approaches that can be taken.

I'm going to put my people to work re-interviewing the key figures involved in the '94 search. We'll also talk to some of the students' friends and teachers. I'd certainly appreciate it if you could make a call to the Leonards: they could have some key information we don't even know about.

My best to Jim—Randy and Sadie, too.
Sincerely,

C. D. Buchanan

Professional Services Center • 2130 Topanga Creek Boulevard • Cummington, VA • 22769-8990
Office: (927) • Local Pager: (927)

THE SEARCH

Below and following: Documents relating to the students' original disappearance in October 1994. Buck Buchanan began focusing his resources on this aspect of the case in February of 1996.

CITY OF BURKITTSVILLE SHERIFF'S DEPARTMENT

Missing Person Affidavit/Verification

Locate/Return ______ DATE TIME **Out of LEAPS/NCIC** ______ REMOVING OFFICER # DATE TIME

NAME OF PERSON REPORTING MISSING/PERSON LOCATED | RELATIONSHIP TO MISSING PERSON | PHONE NUMBER

Name: MICHAEL WILLIAMS **DOB:** 11-9-70 **SS#:** 167-32-1496

Address: 57 FOREST GLEN DRIVE

Missing Since: 10-24-94 **Record #:** MP01

NCIC Reference #:

Missing Person NCIC / LEAPS Categories

☐ **D - Disabled** — A person of any age who is missing and under proven physical/mental disability or is senile, thereby subjecting him/herself or others to personal and immediate danger.

☑ **E - Endangered** — A person of any age who is missing and under circumstances indicating that his/her physical safety may be in danger (including suicidal).

☐ **I - Involuntary** — A person of any age who is missing under circumstances indicating that the disappearance may not have been voluntary (abduction/kidnapping).

☐ **J - Juvenile** — A person who is missing and declared unemancipated as defined by the laws of his/her state of residence and who does not meet any of the criteria set forth in the above listed categories.

☐ **C - Catastrophe Victim** — A person of any age who is missing after a catastrophe.

AFFIDAVIT

I Solemnly swear (or affirm) that the individual named above is declared missing as indicated in the category checked; that his/her whereabouts are unknown; and that upon his/her return, or upon contact with the said missing person, I will immediately notify the Burkittsville Sheriff's Department.

PHONE: [redacted]1100 FAX: [redacted]1137

GREG WILLIAMS
Name of Reporting Party

Street Address of Reporting Party

City / Town State Zip Code

Home Phone of Reporting Party

Work Phone of Reporting Party

FATHER
Relationship of Reporting Party to Missing Person

Greg Williams
Signature of Reporting Party

RON CRAVENS | B68 | 10-24-94 | 5:16 A.M. / (P.M.)
Officer Taking Report | Pers # | Date of Report | Time of Report

BURKITTSVILLE SHERIFF'S OFFICE

Ronald Cravens, Sheriff

October 26, 1994
FOR IMMEDIATE RELEASE

Agents from the Federal Bureau of Investigation (FBI) and the Maryland State Police have officially joined the Burkittsville Sheriff's Office in the search for missing Montgomery College students Heather Donahue, Joshua Leonard, and Michael Williams. The three students, formally declared missing on October 24, 1994, were last seen by two fishermen on the morning of October 21, 1994 as they hiked into the Black Hills Forest just outside Burkittsville.

"We're grateful for the assistance," declared Sheriff Ron Cravens. "At this point, we're trying to cover a pretty big area." Cravens also announced the FBI hopes to bring in high-technology search equipment, such as infra-red detectors and helicopters and cameras tied to the national GPS system. "The weather will be a key factor in determining how much of that equipment we can bring to bear in the search for these kids." As of 9:00 a.m. EST, the National Weather Service was forecasting cloudy skies and possible thunderstorms for the Black Hills area.

The Burkittsville Sheriff's Office will continue to coordinate all search operations: media contact will be coordinated through a special liaison officer to be brought in by the FBI.

To date, close to three dozen local volunteers have also joined the search, which has been operating continuously since the evening of October 24. Sheriff Cravens urges anyone in the community who is able to assist to phone his office for instructions on how to join the search party.

MISSING

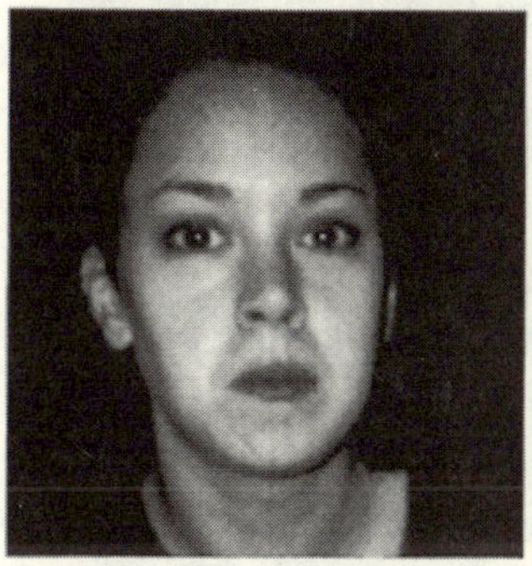

Heather Donahue
Age: 22 Height: 5'6" Weight: 127lb
Eyes: hazel Hair: brown

Joshua Leonard
Age: 23 Height: 5'10" Weight: 152lb
Eyes: blue Hair: blond

Michael Williams
Age: 24 Height: 5'8" Weight: 169lb
Eyes: brown Hair: brown

Last seen camping in the Black Hills Forest area, near Burkittsville.

PLEASE CALL FREDERICK COUNTY SHERIFF'S OFFICE WITH ANY INFORMATION YOU MAY HAVE!

(240)

This flyer—originally posted in Burkittsville and surrounding towns on October 28, 1994—was redistributed with the discovery of the students' footage in October of 1995. Over the next six months, more than 100,000 copies were proliferated among law-enforcement personnel and missing children's groups nationwide. Burkittsville Sheriff Ron Cravens estimates his department received "darn-well several hundred" phone calls concerning possible sightings of the students, from locations as distant as Portland, Oregon.

No significant leads were generated as a result of this flyer.

BUCHANAN'S
PRIVATE INVESTIGATIVE AGENCY, INC.
Serving Since 1940

This Report Constitutes Confidential Work Product and May Further Constitute Work Product of the Nature of an Attorney-Client Privilege

February 26, 1996
Re: BPIA #94-117
Transcript of Tape 94-117-11
Transcript of a conversation between Frank Lauriat and Buck Buchanan on February 23, 1996.

Investigator Buchanan: All right. Can you repeat that?

Frank Lauriat: Okay. I've been talking to sources within the Bureau about the original search. They were all very impressed with how Cravens went about it—he did a thorough job. One of the agents faxed me a map—here, hold on a second. [Sound of rustling paper.] Yeah, Cravens did it right: split the whole area into a grid, real textbook-style search. This agent didn't think you'd find anything he overlooked.

IB: Okay.

FL: I had a thought. Well, a couple thoughts actually. Could you turn it off for a second?

IB: Hold on.

************************* [recorder is shut off]

FL: The other idea was to look at any suspected felons who might have been in the area at the time. Call the state cops in Virginia, West Virginia, Pennsylvania—the whole Northeast region.

IB: We're already on the state thing—Sonenberg is cross-checking names from the most wanted lists against a list of camping permits the Park Ranger gave us. How about the bureau's list from ninety-four?

FL: I can get that and fax it over to you. I'll give you a couple years before, couple years after, too.

IB: Great.

FL: Why don't you try talking to Cravens?

IB: He's not returning my calls. We're going to go at that information through Hart.

FL: He's the deputy?

IB: That's right.

Professional Services Center • 2130 Topanga Creek Boulevard • Cummington, VA • 22769-8990
Office: (927) • Local Pager: (927)

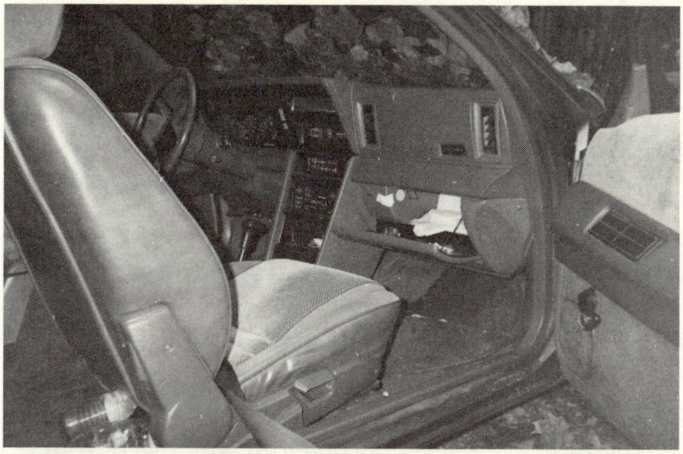

Official crime-scene photo of the inside passenger seat of the students' car, found on October 25, 1994. The glove box was opened by the police—the interior of the vehicle had been undisturbed.

Forensic scientists discerned that the car had been left abandoned for four to five days. Though the ground was moist during this period, no footprints leading to or from the vehicle could be located.

Several volunteers, including a few pictured with bloodhounds, aided local, state, and federal law-enforcement officials. Separate search teams combed the Black Hills Forest for over a week in the search for the missing students.

From the October 31st Frederick Post.

Students Disappearance Echoes Old Legends

by RODMAN JENKINS
Staff Reporter

BURKITTSVILLE -- As children throughout the Frederick area prepare for Halloween, you can be sure that mixed in among the stories of vampires, ghosts, and werewolves being whispered to them by parents and older siblings are tales of Maryland's most famous supernatural resident -- the Blair Witch.

"Every kid around here knows the story," says Bill Barnes, director of the Burkittsville Historical Society. "When I was growing up, my brother used to terrify me with tales of the old woman in the woods. It made me scared to go into the general store in town, because there was an old lady working behind the counter there who looked exactly like a witch."

The Blair Witch tale, appropriately enough, does start with the story of an old woman. In the late 1700s, according to Barnes, Elly Kedward was banished from the town of Blair for drawing blood from some of the local children. Soon after, some of those children started disappearing. Fearing for their lives, the townspeople abandoned their village. Burkittsville was founded on the site of Blair in 1824. Several other mysterious disappearances attributed to the Blair Witch have occurred over the years.

Then, in 1940, the local folklore turned deadly. Over the course of two years, a hermit named Rustin Parr, who lived out in the Black Hills forest, kidnapped and murdered seven Burkittsville children before turning himself into police. According to Parr, the Blair Witch told him to do it.

Now, with the disappearance last week of three Montgomery College students, Sheriff Ron Cravens of Burkittsville wants to make sure people understand the difference between fantasy and reality.

"The Blair Witch tales are all in good fun," he said. "What we don't want people thinking is that there's another Rustin Parr wandering around out there in the woods." Barnes echoed the Sheriff's sentiments. "There's no reason that (continued on page A6)

BUCHANAN'S
PRIVATE INVESTIGATIVE AGENCY, INC.
Serving Since 1940

This Report Constitutes Confidential Work Product and May Further Constitute Work Product of the Nature of an Attorney-Client Privilege

February 26, 1996
Re: BPIA #94-117

Transcript of Tape 94-117-14

Carlos Sonenberg: Do you mind if I record this?

Bill Barnes: Not at all.

CS: So tell me about the Blair Witch.

BB: What do you want to know?

CS: What you think about the legend—all the mysterious events that have happened over the years.

BB: I don't think the Blair Witch has anything to do with what happened to those students, if that's what you're asking.

CS: That's part of what I'm asking. So what about the footage?

BB: Well . . . I know you're working for that girl's mother, but I have to say, I think it's all a hoax.

CS: Because . . . ?

BB: Well, that's what the authorities decided.

CS: But what do you think?

BB: Listen. I've known Ron Cravens all of my life. If he's decided that footage is a hoax, that's good enough for me.

CS: What about the students' disappearance? Is that a hoax?

BB: No. I do think something happened to those kids. Do I think that something was the Blair Witch? No.

CS: So you're a man of science.

BB: I don't believe in the supernatural, I guess.

CS: Do you go to church?

BB: That's none of your business.

CS: I'm sorry. I didn't mean the question to be offensive.

BB: What does any of this have to do with the missing students?

CS: It has to do with admitting certain possibilities into this case.

BB: [laughter] You want to track down the Blair Witch?

CS: I want to track down anyone—and anything—that might be involved in those kids' disappearance.

Professional Services Center • 2130 Topanga Creek Boulevard • Cummington, VA • 22769-8990
Office: (927) [redacted] • Local Pager: (927) [redacted]

Burkittsville Historical Society's Bill Barnes

BUCHANAN'S
PRIVATE INVESTIGATIVE AGENCY, INC.
Serving Since 1940

This Report Constitutes Confidential Work Product and May Further Constitute Work Product of the Nature of an Attorney-Client Privilege

February 28, 1996
Re: BPIA #94-117

To: Buck Buchanan

From: Carlos Sonenberg

Re: Barnes/Johnson/Blair Witch

I spoke with Barnes at the Burkittsville Historical Society. He was the one who was all over the media back when the students disappeared.

He gave me a mountain of stuff on witchcraft, including a videotape made in the 1970s, which I found particularly interesting. I'm including transcriptions of the relevant parts, which all come from the mouth of a supposed "witch" named Lucan Johnson (and I always thought a male witch was called a warlock).

Note the mention of "The Blair Witch Cult." Echoes of Jim Jones/David Koresh?

I'll have to find out what this is.

> ". . . the most famous cases of witchcraft? In England, there was Lady Alice Kidderly, and Elizabeth Sawyer . . . here in America, you have the Blair Witch in Maryland . . . her name was Elly Kedward, and the story goes that she had bled a few children with some pinpricks. She was tried, convicted, and banished to the forest . . . that winter was supposedly one of the harshest ever, and everyone assumed she died.
>
> "The following winter, though, over half the town's children disappeared . . . ever since then, it seems as if whenever anything out of the ordinary happens in that area, people blame it on the Blair Witch, especially after publication of The Blair Witch Cult . . . this book was a sensationalized version of the case, almost a "how-to-be-a-witch" manual, which was completely fictional, totally sensationalized . . ."
>
> ". . . witchcraft is a scientific study of energies and materials . . . witchcraft is focusing energy on specific goals, it's neither intrinsically good or evil. The practice is called Wiccannism—for all intents and purposes, it's a new religion, reborn back in the 1940s, though its origins go back to pre-Christian Europe. But we lost most of the records during the burning times . . ."

"... we use natural lore, what you might call herbalism. It's a well-known fact that most medicines that are working today are just laboratory-created versions of naturally occurring medicines. Wiccans are similar to early pagans, in that we believe that God is everywhere, in the rocks and trees."

Professional Services Center • 2130 Topanga Creek Boulevard • Cummington, VA • 22769-8990
Office: (927) [redacted] • Local Pager: (927) [redacted]

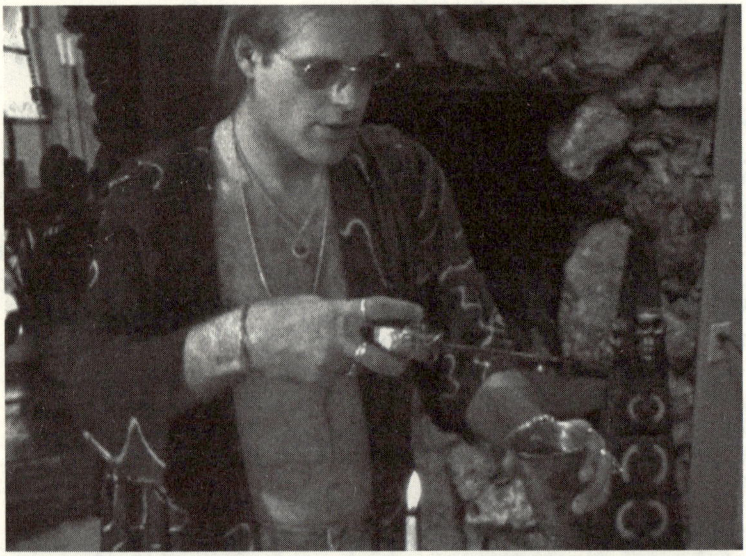

Wiccan believer Lucan Johnson during the 1970s

Bill Combs, being interviewed here by the local media, was one of the many volunteers brought in to help the original search.

BUCHANAN'S
PRIVATE INVESTIGATIVE AGENCY, INC.
Serving Since 1940

This Report Constitutes Confidential Work Product and May Further Constitute Work Product of the Nature of an Attorney-Client Privilege

February 26, 1996
Re: BPIA #94-117
Transcript of Tape 94-117-36

Steve Whately: Could you state your name for the record?

Bill Combs: Bill Combs.

SW: And you understand that this conversation is being taped and will be transcribed at a later date, and do you agree to that taping?

BC: Okay.

SW: Can you describe the search effort to me?

BC: Well, it was pretty intense. The Sheriff—I forget his name—

SW: Ron Cravens.

BC: Yes, Sheriff Cravens, he told us to keep an eye out for anything at all out of the ordinary. There were about twenty-five volunteers that first night, and I remember, we were all standing out in like a military formation, you know? And the Sheriff walked down that line, and introduced himself to each one of us, and said if we saw anything at all, to tell him or one of the other officers about it.

SW: You thought the search was thorough, then.

BC: Oh yeah, I sure did. Everybody out there was really trying as best they could to find those kids.

SW: Do you remember the other volunteers very well?

BC: Well, we were split up into groups of three or four people, so there were a lot of them I never got to meet.

SW: Do you recall anything unusual about any of the volunteers?

BC: No, not really.

SW: Is there anything about what you saw that strikes you, looking back? Something that might not have seemed like evidence at the time, but maybe does now?

BC: Well, gosh, no. We never found any trace of those kids, nothing at all. I guess that's the only odd thing, because we sure went over that forest pretty thoroughly.

SW: Okay. Thanks for talking to me, Bill.

BC: You're welcome.

Professional Services Center • 2130 Topanga Creek Boulevard • Cummington, VA • 22769-8990
Office: (927) ███ • Local Pager: (927) ███

BUCHANAN'S
PRIVATE INVESTIGATIVE AGENCY, INC.
Serving Since 1940

This Report Constitutes Confidential Work Product and May Further Constitute Work Product of the Nature of an Attorney-Client Privilege

Steve Whately: Could you state your name for the record?

Emily McKenna: Emily McKenna.

SW: And you understand that this conversation is being taped and will be transcribed at a later date, all of which you had previously agreed to.

EM: That's what you told me before?

SW: That's right.

EM: I understand.

SW: And you agree.

EM: I do.

SW: Emily, you volunteered to join the search party formed in October 1994 to find Heather Donahue, Michael Williams, and Joshua Leonard, is that right?

EM: I sure did.

SW: Do you remember that search?

EM: Oh yes.

SW: Can you tell me about it?

EM: Yeah. Problem with that search was, nobody was looking for those kids in the right place.

SW: Really?

EM: Yes, really. I kept tellin' 'em they should look at this old house I know in the woods, 'cause everybody knows that's the Blair Witch house.

SW: The Blair Witch?

EM: Yeah. [laughter] Now you're playing dumb with me, ain't you?

SW: Maybe. Why don't you tell me about the Blair Witch?

EM: Blair Witch is what got those kids.

SW: Got 'em?

EM: Killed 'em, I mean. Damn, you ain't really that dumb, are you?

SW: What makes you think the Blair Witch killed those students?

EM: I seen some of the film.

SW: You don't think it's a hoax?

EM: Sure don't. Those kids went out there lookin' for trouble, and trouble sure enough found 'em.

SW: Let's go back to the search for a minute, Emily. Did you see anything at all out there that struck you as a clue?

EM: Hell, of course not. I just told you, we weren't lookin' in the right place.

SW: Okay . . . How many nights were you out there?

EM: Two. After the second night, Cravens told me they didn't need me no more.

SW: Do you know if they ever went to this Blair Witch house?

EM: I doubt it. Cravens is a real tight-ass. He don't want to hear nothing that don't fit in with his narrow view of the world. Hell, he'd ignore the Blair Witch if she walked right up to him and kicked him in the balls. [laughter] He just don't have his mind open, that's all.

Professional Services Center • 2130 Topanga Creek Boulevard • Cummington, VA • 22769-8990
Office: (927) ■■■■ • Local Pager: (927) ■■■■

After persistent requests, Emily McKenna finally agreed to let her picture be published in this book.

BUCHANAN'S
PRIVATE INVESTIGATIVE AGENCY, INC.
Serving Since 1940

This Report Constitutes Confidential Work Product and May Further Constitute Work Product of the Nature of an Attorney-Client Privilege

February 25, 1996
Re: BPIA #94-117
Transcript of Tape 94-117-43

Steve Whately: Could you please state your name for the record?

Deputy Leonard Callihan: Leonard Callihan. I'm a Deputy with the Burkittsville Sheriff's Department.

SW: Deputy, you understand that this conversation is being taped and will be transcribed at a later date, and you agree to that taping?

LC: I do.

SW: I want to say first of all, I appreciate your talking to me.

LC: You're welcome.

SW: I'd like to ask you a couple questions regarding the original search for the missing Montgomery College students.

LC: Go ahead.

SW: Sheriff Cravens organized and ran the entire operation?

LC: He was tactical.

SW: Can you describe your role in the search?

LC: I implemented the sheriff's plan.

SW: Specifically . . .

LC: I coordinated the different search groups, brought in the dog teams. When the State Police and FBI came on board, I was liaison.

SW: Were you involved directly in the search?

LC: Every night.

SW: All ten nights of the search?

LC: That's correct.

SW: That seems like a lot to handle.

LC: That's my job. What's your question?

SW: All right . . . In retrospect, do you think there's anything that could have been done differently during that original search?

LC: Can we go off the record?

SW: Of course.

****************[recorder is switched back on]

SW: Let me turn to the search party volunteers for a minute. Did any of them appear at all suspicious to you?

LC: No.

SW: Why was the decision made not to use some of the equipment the FBI brought in?

LC: The weather was a factor.

SW: Were there other factors?

LC: Let's go off the record again.

[Interview ends]

Professional Services Center • 2130 Topanga Creek Boulevard • Cummington, VA • 22769-8990
Office: (927) ████ • Local Pager: (927) ████

Deputy Leonard Callihan's efforts were instrumental during the original search for the missing students.

BUCHANAN'S

PRIVATE INVESTIGATIVE AGENCY, INC.

Serving Since 1940

This Report Constitutes Confidential Work Product and May Further Constitute Work Product of the Nature of an Attorney-Client Privilege

March 4, 1996

Re: BPIA #94-117

TO: FILE

FROM: CDB

RE: TRANSCRIBED ANSWERING MACHINE MESSAGE

Hey Buck, it's Steve Whately. It's just after midnight on February 28th—no, it's the 29th now, isn't it—goddamnit, I'm going crazy here! I'm calling you from a Sunoco truck stop right outside of Allentown.

I just about drove off the damn road. I was listening to the interview tapes in the car, and something hit me like a ton of bricks. I'm talking to Hart about the search party, and he was saying how by Thursday night—that's the 27th—they were on their second go-round through the forest. But Buck, they should have found those kids, because according to that footage Mrs. Donahue's got, they were still out there, wandering around lost, all three of them. Do you have a copy of the girl's journal pages? I think that ties in with what the girl was writing too.

Makes me think that either Cravens was right, and the footage is faked, or . . .

Or I don't know what. Jesus. Am I making sense here? Maybe you figured this out before—I sure as hell didn't. All right—I'll be in New York all day tomorrow testifying. Leave a message with my service, let me know when I can get hold of you so we can talk about this. All right, I'll talk to you later.

Professional Services Center • 2130 Topanga Creek Boulevard • Cummington, VA • 22769-8990

Office: (927) ████ • Local Pager: (927) ████

Mary Brown is a Burkittsville local whom most residents regard as a reclusive eccentric. However, her conversations with both the students and Buck Buchanan's investigative team yielded some pertinent information.

Ed Swanson (left) and his father-in-law, Bob Griffin, warned the students about venturing into the forest.

BUCHANAN'S

PRIVATE INVESTIGATIVE AGENCY, INC.

Serving Since 1940

This Report Constitutes Confidential Work Product and May Further Constitute Work Product of the Nature of an Attorney-Client Privilege

February 26, 1996
Re: BPIA #94-117
Transcript of Tape 94-117-100

Buck Buchanan (CDB): I'm stating for the record that this conversation is being recorded for investigative purposes, with the understanding that it will be transcribed and a copy of that transcription provided to my client for her information. Is that your understanding?

Mary Brown: Yes, it is.

CDB: Could you state your name for the record?

MB: Mary Brown.

CDB: Mary, I'm showing you a picture here of three Montgomery College students. Do you recognize any of these students?

MB: Well, sure. These are the ones who talked to me, like I told you before.

CDB: You know that a few days after they talked to you, these students were reported missing?

MB: I read the papers.

CDB: Have you seen these students since?

MB: That one—that boy. I've seen him. The one with the beard.

CDB: That's Joshua Leonard.

MB: I know that.

CDB: Mary, I'm looking at a copy of a report taken by Sheriff Ron Cravens after he talked with you in December of 1994.

MB: That's when I saw him, all right.

CDB: And you called Sheriff Cravens?

MB: I did. I told the sheriff they had to find that boy, because he was in terrible pain.

CDB: That's what I don't understand about this report. It says you saw Joshua, but he wasn't really here, he was someplace else?

MB: That's what I told the sheriff. I saw an apparition of him, an image. He was standing right outside the door to my trailer, right where you are. And he was screaming something awful.

CDB: Why was he screaming?

MB: He was in terrible pain. He was missing some teeth and holding onto his side, and his hands were all wet and oh, it was terrible.

CDB: Why do you think he came to you?

MB: I don't have any idea about that.

CDB: Did he say anything to you?

MB: No. He was just crying. He couldn't speak.

CDB: When the students first talked to you, did you and Joshua speak at all?

MB: No. We didn't talk. The girl did all the talking. She was asking about the Blair Witch.

CDB: When you saw Joshua on December 23rd, did he look the same as he did two months previously?

MB: Well, no. He was an apparition, I told you that.

CDB: Thank you, Mary.

Professional Services Center • 2130 Topanga Creek Boulevard • Cummington, VA • 22769-8990
Office: (927) ██████ • Local Pager: (927) ██████

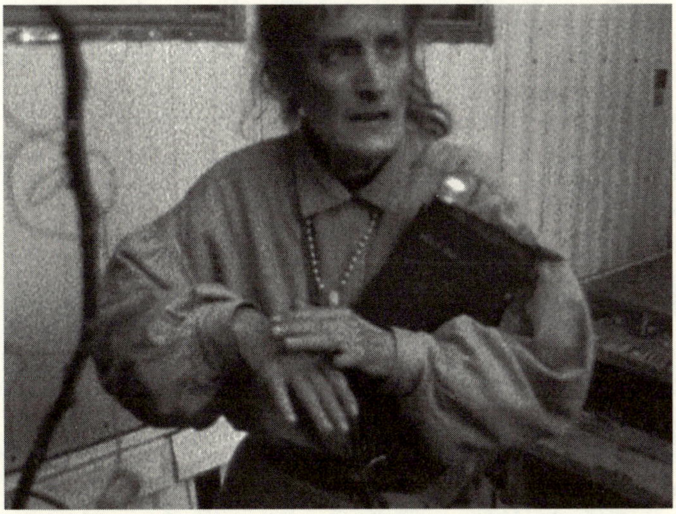

BUCHANAN'S

PRIVATE INVESTIGATIVE AGENCY, INC.

Serving Since 1940

This Report Constitutes Confidential Work Product and May Further Constitute Work Product of the Nature of an Attorney-Client Privilege

February 26, 1996
Re: BPIA #94-117
Transcript of Tape 94-117-102

Buck Buchanan (CDB): I'm stating for the record that this conversation is being recorded for investigative purposes, with the understanding that it will be transcribed and a copy of that transcription provided to my client for her information. Is that your understanding?

Bob Griffin: Yes sir, it is.

CDB: Why don't you state your name for the record now?

BG: My name is Bob Griffin. I'm the last one to see those kids alive.

CDB: Thank you, Mr. Griffin. Why don't you tell me about that morning when you saw them?

BG: Jesus. Don't you want to ask me something else? I feel like I've been over this a hundred times already.

CDB: I appreciate you doing it once more. So do the kids' families, I know.

BG: Yeah. Well, I was fishing with my son-in-law—that's Ed Swanson—up in the Creek. That's Tappy East Creek.

CDB: Tappy East, all right.

BG: And here come these three college kids, hiking along with their backpacks and their high-tech film stuff. They asked me about the Blair Witch, I told 'em, and then they walked off into the woods.

CDB: And you never saw those kids again?

BG: Hell, no. Nobody did.

CDB: Do you remember anything at all unusual about what they were wearing? Anything distinctive come to your mind?

BG: What they were wearing? Jesus, I don't know what they were wearing.

CDB: All right. Did they say anything about where they were going?

BG: They were going to find the Blair Witch, that's what I remember. I told 'em not to do that. The Beanpole'll tell you that.

CDB: Beanpole?

BG: Ed. You talk to him yet?

CDB: No, I haven't.

BG: Well, he'll tell you the same thing. I knew those kids were asking for trouble. Told 'em so myself.

Professional Services Center • 2130 Topanga Creek Boulevard • Cummington, VA • 22769-8990
Office: (927) [redacted] • Local Pager: (927) [redacted]

March 27,

Dear Buck,

Something very strange happened today. Sheriff Cravens stopped by the house and dropped off Heather's journal.

I haven't spoken with the man in weeks, ever since I called him all those names in newspapers. In fact, after the law suit, I never thought I'd hear from him again, and there he is, standing on my doorstep, handing me what could be my baby girl's last words on Earth. I didn't know what to say, and I told him just that.

"You could say thank you," he told me. So I thanked him, but he didn't even smile at me, or tip his hat, or say you're welcome.

Then I asked him about the footage, and it was like a curtain went down in front of his eyes.

"We're going to hold onto that," he told me. And the way he said it, like he was almost sorry about it – I forgot to get angry.

Sometimes I have the feeling that man is hiding an awful lot of secrets.

With regard to the investigation, I appreciate your concern, but let me state it here again for the record: money is no object.

You do what you think best: if that means reviewing every piece of paper Sheriff Cravens has filled out since 1981, you do that. Take all the time you want. All Jim and I care about is finding Heather.

We do so appreciate your help.

Sincerely,

Angela Donahue

THE STUDENTS

Heather Donahue, Michael Williams, and Joshua Leonard—the day before their disappearance.

Inevitably, as Buck Buchanan began investigating the students' disappearance, he and his team found themselves probing into the past for clues. Investigator Jen Colton was assigned to interview Heather, Josh, and Michael's friends: because she was roughly their age, Buck felt they might open up more readily to her.

BUCHANAN'S
PRIVATE INVESTIGATIVE AGENCY, INC.
Serving Since 1940

March 4, 1996

Clark Wissler
President
Montgomery College
51 Mannakee Street
Rockville, MD 20850

Dear President Wissler:

I want to thank you again for all the cooperation you, your staff, and your students showed me last week. I know how difficult it must have been for all of you to relive those horrible days when Heather, Josh, and Michael first disappeared. The one consolation I can offer is the hope that somehow what we're doing will help bring peace of mind and closure to this case, for the sake of all the students' friends and families.

Sincerely,

Jennifer Colton

Jennifer Colton
Investigative Associate

Professional Services Center • 2130 Topanga Creek Boulevard • Cummington, VA • 22769-8990
Office: (927) [redacted] • Local Pager: (927) [redacted]

HEATHER DONAHUE

Heather apparently wrote this biographical sketch of herself to accompany her thesis project.

Born on August 17, 1972, Heather Donahue lived most of her life in New York City. Virtually every summer, however, she would visit with her grandparents, Randy and Sadie Donahue, who lived in Frederick County, Maryland. Some of Heather's earliest memories are of her grandfather's tales of the ghosts and witches said to haunt the area. She made it her mission to investigate and document the origins of these stories, primarily as an act of preservation.

Once her family moved to Maryland in 1991, Heather began studying video production at Montgomery College in Rockville. She worked as a videographer for countless weddings and bar mitzvahs, simultaneously planning her first major project, a documentary on the story of her grandfather's that both fascinated and frightened her the most—the legend of the Blair Witch.

It was Randy Donahue who first told his granddaughter Heather tales of Elly Kedward and the history of Burkittsville, sparking her interest in the legend of the Blair Witch.

Heather's best friend, Rachel Meyer.

Professor Michael DeCoto encouraged Heather to pursue her thesis in his film class.

BUCHANAN'S
PRIVATE INVESTIGATIVE AGENCY, INC.

Serving Since 1940

This Report Constitutes Confidential Work Product and May Further Constitute Work Product of the Nature of an Attorney-Client Privilege

February 26, 1996
Re: BPIA #94-117

Transcript of Tape 94-117-53

Jennifer Colton: For the record, can you state your name?

Rachel Meyer: Rachel Meyer.

JC: And you consent to the taping and transcription of this interview, Rachel?

RM: I do.

JC: Everyone I've talked to says that you were Heather's best friend.

RM: Oh yeah, I was.

JC: So tell me about her.

RM: You mean—

JC: What kind of person she was, what she liked to do, who she hung out with.

RM: Well, she was a good person. A good friend. We used to talk all the time.

JC: Who were her other friends?

RM: She was pretty close to another girl in her film class named Theresa Burkhart. I could give you her number.

JC: That would be great.

RM: I know she stayed pretty friendly with one of the three Kathys. I can't remember which one.

JC: The three Kathys?

RM: These three girls named Kathy from high school. They all used to sit together—I think the one Heather knew was Kathy Seaton. I'll give you her number too.

JC: Okay. What about boyfriends? Did she have one?

RM: There was a guy named Gregg something-or-other that she was seeing, but I don't think it was serious. Heather just wasn't into that. I mean, she dated a little. She went to our prom with this guy named Peter Stanton, and they went out for the whole summer between high school and college. Then he went up to UMass, and that was that.

JC: I know you've probably answered this question a hundred times, but can you think of anyone who would have wanted to hurt her?

RM: No. I really can't. And I have thought about it a lot.

JC: Let's go back to 1994, to those few weeks leading up to her film shoot. What was on Heather's mind?

RM: Finding a sound guy. [laughter] That was what was on her mind the whole summer.

JC: She was preoccupied?

RM: Completely obsessed, more like it. The film was all she talked about. Truthfully, we kind of drifted apart a little those last few weeks—I was interning at the paper, and she was getting all the background material together on her film.

JC: On the Blair Witch?

RM: Yeah, on the Blair Witch.

JC: The way you say it, it seems that you don't believe in the Blair Witch.

RM: What rational person does? Hey, I'm from New Orleans, and I've been around that voodoo stuff my whole life, and I've seen a million and one of those tarot readers and fortune tellers, and I've never seen a single one of them that wasn't entirely fake. Heather, on the other hand, was completely into that stuff. Ouija boards, tarot cards—you name it, she had it.

JC: Did Heather seem troubled about anything those last few weeks?

RM: Not at all. Except finding a sound guy, like I said. Hey, can I ask you a question?

JC: Sure.

RM: Do you think that after all this time you're still going to find her alive?

JC: Well. . . .

RM: You don't, do you?

JC: Well, you know that old baseball saying, right? It ain't over—

RM: Till it's over.

JC: Right.

RM: Who thought that saying up, anyway?

JC: I think it was Yogi Berra. He used to play for the Yankees.

RM: Yogi Bear? [laughter]

JC: No, Yogi Berra.

RM: That's a pretty stupid saying.

JC: Well, maybe. But in cases like this one, it's usually true. Until we find out what really happened, we don't rule anything out.

RM: Keep hope alive, right? [laughter] Jesse Jackson.

JC: Right, Jesse Jackson.

RM: Jesus. I can't believe I'm laughing about this.

JC: That's all right, Rachel. Thanks for talking to me.

RM: You're welcome.

Professional Services Center • 2130 Topanga Creek Boulevard • Cummington, VA • 22769-8990
Office: (927) ████ • Local Pager: (927) ████

Buck Buchanan and Randy Donahue originally met in 1982, when Buck was hired to do a security analysis at the local airport where Randy worked. During Buck's month-long assignment, the two became friends.

BUCHANAN'S
PRIVATE INVESTIGATIVE AGENCY, INC.
Serving Since 1940

This Report Constitutes Confidential Work Product and May Further Constitute Work Product of the Nature of an Attorney-Client Privilege

February 29, 1996
Re: BPIA #94-117
Transcript of Tape 94-117-104

Buck Buchanan (CDB): I'm stating for the record that this conversation is being recorded for investigative purposes, with the understanding that it will be transcribed and a copy of that transcription provided to my client for her information. Is that your understanding?

Randy Donahue: Sure thing.

CDB: Could you state your name for the record?

RD: Randy Donahue.

CDB: Randy, tell me a little about your granddaughter Heather. Were the two of you close?

RD: We were. Not so much when they lived in New York, but when they moved back here, yes.

CDB: When was the last time you saw Heather?

RD: The weekend before she left. We all had dinner together.

CDB: What was her state of mind then?

RD: Oh, she was very happy. Very much looking forward to doing her movie.

CDB: She didn't seem worried about anything?

RD: No, not at all.

CDB: Do you have any idea what might have happened to her?

RD: I don't like to think about that too much.

CDB: But when you do . . .

RD: I think about somebody—or something—running around out there in those woods. I think about all the crazies in this world.

CDB: I'm asking if you think about anybody specific—anybody you know of who might have had reason to hurt Heather.

RD: That's what I'm getting up to. Somebody specific.

CDB: Are you all right? You want a drink?

RD: Hell, no. I don't want a drink. Buck, listen. You and I sit here in broad daylight, in these comfortable chairs, with the phone right there, and the Crottys right next door, and we feel like we're in charge of the world. But there's something out there in those woods that don't play by our rules.

CDB: The Blair Witch.

RD: Yes. Now don't look at me like I'm crazy. I've seen stuff out there in those woods you wouldn't believe. When I was growing up . . .

CDB: Go on.

RD: Hell, you're going to think I've gone senile on you.

CDB: Jesus, Randy. I know you're senile, don't worry about that. [laughter] Tell me what you saw.

RD: Well, all right. When I was a boy—before they ran Black Rock Road smack through the middle of the forest—you used to be able to pick up this little trail right in the center of Burkittsville, and follow it straight up to Tappy East Creek. There was this swimming hole up there that me and my friends used to go to all the time. Anyway, one afternoon, middle of the summer, I must have been twelve, maybe thirteen, and none of my friends were around, so—

CDB: So you snuck off by yourself.

RD: Yeah. Now the old folks were always telling us what happened to Robin Weaver—you know that story?

CDB: Yes.

RD: Well, they were always warning us kids not to go into the woods, that the Witch would get us. But you know how it is—you don't believe it, and then you go out there and nothing happens, and so you eventually ignore what they tell you altogether, and you forget to be careful. So this one afternoon, I'm hiking along the trail by myself—and you have to understand that this trail is some pretty tough going, it's right in the middle of the forest and all overgrown—and I'm just trying to make sure the branches of the trees don't snap back and hit me in the face as I push 'em past. And I come to this big pine tree, with a huge branch right in the middle of the trail. When I push it back, somebody grabs it. And it's this old woman, standin' right there on the trail, holding that branch, staring at me. Jesus. I've never been so scared in my life. You know, it's been about seventy years and I'm gettin' goddamn goosebumps just thinking about it now. Jesus! It's like I'm still standing there, staring at her. I remember exactly what she looked like.

CDB: So then what happened?

RD: Well my heart is hammering in my chest, and I don't know whether I should scream or laugh because by God is she ugly, she's got hair all over her arms like a lumberjack or something, and she's just staring at me. And then she says "Donahue."

CDB: And?

RD: What do you mean "and"? That was enough for me. I turned around and ran like holy hell. How did she know my name? I'd never seen her before.

CDB: Well, to me—

RD: I know. It sounds like I just came across some crazy old woman in the forest. But I tell you, I've heard other people talk about her too—people a lot older than me, a lot younger. And she always looks the same. It was the Blair Witch, Buck.

CDB: And that's who you think got Heather?

RD: That's who Heather went out to find. I guess you could say it's my fault she went out there, because I told her all the stories, that one, and—

CDB: Oh, now, cut that out, Randy. What happened to Heather is not your fault.

RD: Well she wouldn't have had the idea to do her film on the Blair Witch if it wasn't for me. Damn it, I just should have kept my mouth shut.

CDB: Don't. Don't do that.

RD: Jesus, Buchanan. Ain't you got no sympathy for an old man?

CDB: You're not that old. And hell yes, you've got my sympathy for Heather's disappearing like this. But that's all. Don't talk to me about any witch.

BUCHANAN'S
PRIVATE INVESTIGATIVE AGENCY, INC.
Serving Since 1940

This Report Constitutes Confidential Work Product and May Further Constitute Work Product of the Nature of an Attorney-Client Privilege

February 29, 1996
Re: BPIA #94-117
Transcript of Tape 94-117-76

Jennifer Colton: For the record, can you state your full name?

Michael DeCoto: Michael DeCoto.

JC: And you consent to the taping and transcription of this interview, Professor DeCoto?

MD: Please, call me Mike.

JC: All right—Mike it is. You consent?

MD: I do.

JC: Heather Donahue was one of your students?

MD: One of my best students. That girl was going places.

JC: Because. . . .

MD: She had drive, and she had real talent. Real strong ideas, and not afraid to express them.

JC: Not afraid to make sure she got her way?

MD: No.

JC: Did that make her any enemies?

MD: No, no—not at all. I'm not talking strong in her personal interactions, you see. I'm talking about film.

JC: So you can't think of anyone who might have wanted to hurt her?

MD: Not at all.

JC: You've seen the footage that showed up last year?

MD: I have.

JC: What can you tell me about that?

MD: It looks like she was off to a good start—I mean, that sounds cold to say, but with the exception of some of the camera work, I think it would have made a really good film.

JC: It's not a hoax, in your opinion.

MD: Of course not. That's the film Heather wanted to make. Whatever was happening to her out there. . . . I don't know anything about that.

JC: You verified for the police that the film they found was the same film Heather bought from the school?

MD: I did.

JC: And you gave them a copy of her thesis?

MD: Yes.

JC: I wonder if I can get a copy as well.

MD: I suppose. If it's all right with the family.

JC: The family's who I'm working for. But I'll have them call you.

MD: Okay.

JC: Good. Can you talk about Joshua Leonard for a minute?

Professional Services Center • 2130 Topanga Creek Boulevard • Cummington, VA • 22769-8990
Office: (927) [redacted] • Local Pager: (927) [redacted]

The front page of Heather's film class thesis along with her professor's comments.

THE BLAIR WITCH PROJECT

PROPOSAL FOR A STUDENT FILM THESIS

SUBMITTED APRIL 18, 1994 BY

HEATHER DONAHUE

OVERVIEW: Western Maryland is home to one of the most enduring of all American folk legends—the Blair Witch. Since the late 1700s, there have been a number of disturbing incidents involving the disappearance of children from the Burkittsville area, all of which have been attributed to the Blair Witch.

My documentary will tell the story of the Blair Witch, trying to separate the known facts from the legend that has grown up around them. The heart of my film will be a weekend journey into the Black Hills Forest, the physical location for many of the legend's most famous incidents.

On-camera interviews will be intercut with footage of my journey, and form a significant portion of the film. Among those I will speak to:

Burkittsville Natives

Local Law Enforcement Officials on the Rustin Parr Case (Parr was a serial killer in the 1940s who murdered seven children on the supposed "instructions" of the Blair Witch)

Folklore Experts, including Bill Barnes of the Burkittsville Historical Society

I will need a sound person and a DP. I have approached Theresa Burkhart and Joshua Leonard, and both seem interested in the project.

I plan to film in 16mm black and white to create a more evocative piece. Filming will take place immediately after summer break, depending on people's schedules and availability.

Good idea, Heather – come speak with me about SP, DP. :)

TO: BUCK001@[redacted]

FROM: RESEARCHSEARCH@[redacted]

DATE: March 4, 1996

RE: BINGO

Buck—

I think I've got something.

We know the reason the Donahues moved from New York was because the father got tired of doing the prosecuting attorney thing in New York, right? Well guess which trial convinced him he'd had enough? Bud DiGrassi's.

It turns out Donahue was one of the guys who helped put DiGrassi away for good in 1989. Nobody made any overt threats toward him, but Donahue just got tired of dealing with all of the sleaze. I think Angela had had enough of the city by then, anyway. His folks were from down near Frederick, so that's how they ended up in Maryland.

Flash-forward to 1992. DiGrassi's in jail, and he gets cancer. Terminal. They won't let him out to be with his family—hell, they had such a hard time locking him up, who can blame them? It takes the guy nine months to die.

That's when Bud, Jr. goes apeshit. Swears how everybody involved with putting his dad in jail is a killer, and he's the tough guy that's going to make them pay.

In September of 1994, the head of the parole board gets whacked—gangland-style, one bullet to the head—while he's sitting in a parking lot, waiting for his wife to finish grocery shopping.

In July last year, Donahue's ex-boss Thauheimer is found dead of what looks like a heart attack. By this point, the cops are looking high and low for Bud, Jr., who is nowhere to be found.

Then two weeks ago, Thauheimer's daughter is walking back to her dorm at NYU when somebody steps up behind her, and puts a gun to her head. A NYC beat cop chooses that particular moment to walk out of a deli right behind them, and he disarms gunman #1.

Gunman #1 turns out to be Bud, Jr.—who's apparently decided the sins of the fathers carry down to the next generation.

Junior's now sitting out at Rikers, while they prepare to charge him for attempted murder. Should I go check him out?

—Sonenberg

TO: RESEARCHSEARCH@[redacted]

FROM: BUCK001@[redacted]

DATE: March 4, 1996

RE: BINGO

Give me a heads-up the next time you send me an e-mail—you know I don't check this thing very often.

Whately's in New York already. I put him on DiGrassi.

Good work.

—Buck

Bud DiGrassi, Jr., photographed by the New York Police Department shortly after being arrested for assaulting Brigitte Thauheimer.

BUCHANAN'S
PRIVATE INVESTIGATIVE AGENCY, INC.
Serving Since 1940

This Report Constitutes Confidential Work Product and May Further Constitute Work Product of the Nature of an Attorney-Client Privilege

March 6, 1996
Re: BPIA #94-117

Transcript of Tape 94-117-122

Steven Whately: Would you state your name for the record?

Bud DiGrassi, Jr.: Bud DiGrassi, Jr.

SW: And you understand that this conversation is being taped and will be transcribed at a later date. Do you agree to that taping?

BD: Yeah. Just so long as we're not going to talk about Brigitte Thauheimer. That's what my lawyer told me.

SW: No, we're not going to talk about Brigitte. Let's talk about this girl. Do you recognize her? [Whately hands DiGrassi photograph of Heather]

BD: Yeah.

SW: You do?

BD: Sure, it's your sister, isn't it? I saw her on Tenth Ave last night with the rest of the hookers.

SW: Very funny. You don't know this girl?

BD: No, I don't know her.

SW: Her name is Heather Donahue.

BD: Whoop-de-fucking-doo.

SW: She's been missing since October of 1994.

BD: Yeah? Get me out of here, and I'll help you go look for her.

SW: Did you have anything to do with her disappearance?

BD: Now why the fuck would I care about her?

SW: What about these boys? You recognize them?

BD: No. I don't. What's this all about, anyway?

SW: It's about what happened to these three kids. Their families would like to know. You can appreciate family, right Bud?

BD: Damn fuckin' straight I can. But what makes you think I had anything to do with these kids?

SW: The girl's father is Jim Donahue—the lawyer?

BD: Oh. That asswipe. He was one of the fuckers that railroaded my dad into jail.

SW: Did you kill Heather Donahue?

BD: What?

SW: Did you kill her?

BD: No, I didn't kill her. I never saw her before. You're not gonna pin what happened to them on me.

SW: What happened to them?

BD: Oh no. I'm not playing that game.

SW: Tell you what—you help me out, tell me what you did with the girl and her friends in the woods and I'll put in a good word for you.

BD: I don't need a good word from you, asshole. In October 1994 I was in fucking Italy with my mom, all right? I was helping her get through things after my dad died.

SW: Bet you can prove that, too.

BD: Damn fuckin' straight. You can check my passport.

Professional Services Center • 2130 Topanga Creek Boulevard • Cummington, VA • 22769-8990

Office: (927) ██████ • Local Pager: (927) ██████

JOSHUA LEONARD

Joshua Leonard's biographical sketch from Professor Michael DeCoto's class.

Joshua Leonard began his filmmaking career at 9 years old, documenting local sporting events and family gatherings on his father's 8mm Bell & Howell. Later in his high school years, he wrote and directed his own TV show, "MD. Skunk," which quickly became a local favorite of the Rockville youth culture as well as the highest rated midnight show on WQED cable channel 3. "MD. Skunk" was noted for its unique mixture of skateboarding tricks and punk rock concert footage cleverly edited with stock car chases and classic gun fights.

Joshua later attended and graduated from the television program at Montgomery Community College (MCC). At MCC he learned an array of filmmaking techniques, including on-line Beta editing, basic sound design, 3-point lighting, and 16mm film production.

Joshua is currently working as a commercial videographer for TCI productions and has recently completed directing his own 30-second spot entitled "Nuns With Guns" for The Laugh Factory comedy club and restaurant.

Joshua's latest endeavor is "The Blair Witch Project," a feature-length documentary directed by Heather Donahue. The film explores the folklore and local legends of the occult in Burkittsville and surrounding areas.

BUCHANAN'S

PRIVATE INVESTIGATIVE AGENCY, INC.

Serving Since 1940

This Report Constitutes Confidential Work Product and May Further Constitute Work Product of the Nature of an Attorney-Client Privilege

February 29, 1996
Re: BPIA #94-117

Transcript of Tape 94-117-70

Jennifer Colton: For the record, can you state your name?

Steve Sawyer: Steve Sawyer.

JC: And you consent to the taping and transcription of this interview, Steve?

SS: Yeah, sure. Is this like, anything I say can and will be used against me in a court of law?

JC: No. I'm not a policeman, Steve.

SS: I can see that.

JC: Let's start with the last time you saw Josh.

SS: At B-Side. That's the record store we both worked at.

JC: What date was that?

SS: I don't know exactly. It was a couple days before he left to do his film thing.

JC: What kind of mood was Josh in?

SS: He was loose, you know, relaxed. Josh was a pretty chill guy.

JC: He didn't seem worried about anything?

SS: No. We had a good time.

JC: What did you guys talk about? Did he say anything about the film he was doing?

SS: No. We just hung out. Actually, we smoked.

JC: Smoked?

SS: Some weed, you know.

JC: Okay.

SS: Hey, tell me you never smoked any weed when you were in college.

JC: Was marijuana the only drug Joshua used?

SS: See that's bullshit. You cops all think alike, like marijuana automatically leads you to the hard stuff, which is totally not true. I mean, marijuana is not addictive. It has real health benefits, you know, for cancer patients? They've done studies.

JC: Steve, can we stick to the subject?

SS: What? What do you want to know?

JC: I want to know if Josh had any enemies you know about. Was there anyone who might have wanted to hurt him?

SS: I wouldn't know about that.

JC: Could he have been into anyone for any money?

SS: You mean like a dealer, or something. No, no way. Deep down, see, Josh was a real nerd. Weed was all he did. He only did it to relax, you know. Like we'd go over to his house and hang in the basement and smoke and watch "2001: A Space Odyssey." That was his favorite film.

JC: All right, Steve. Thanks.

SS: Is that it?

JC: Yes. I think we're finished here.

Professional Services Center • 2130 Topanga Creek Boulevard • Cummington, VA • 22769-8990
Office: (927) ████ • Local Pager: (927) ████

Steve Sawyer on spring break in 1994.

BUCHANAN'S

PRIVATE INVESTIGATIVE AGENCY, INC.

Serving Since 1940

This Report Constitutes Confidential Work Product and May Further Constitute Work Product of the Nature of an Attorney-Client Privilege

February 29, 1996
Re: BPIA #94-117

Transcript of Tape 94-117-76 (continued)
Jennifer Colton with Michael DeCoto

JC: And how would you characterize Joshua?

MD: He seemed like a bit of a lost soul to me, really.

JC: What do you mean?

MD: Well, it was obvious he loved movies. But it was equally obvious he had no real passion for the craft of film-making. I think he was just taking my course because he thought it would be a cool thing to do.

JC: Was he friendly with the other students?

MD: Josh was very popular. I think he worked on virtually every student's film that previous semester.

JC: That sounds like passion to me.

MD: Well, again, I have to distinguish between the craft and the work.

JC: I see. Let me ask you a couple more questions about Josh. How did he seem that week before the filming?

MD: I can't say that I noticed anything out of the ordinary—but that was a year and a half ago at this point. And I'm not sure I noticed his frame of mind all that closely anyway.

JC: Did you ever hear Josh talk about his home life at all?

MD: No.

JC: Did he ever talk about a boy named Steve Sawyer?

MD: No.

JC: Anything at all he said about work?

MD: Work?

JC: His job. He worked at a record store.

MD: I see. I didn't know that.

JC: And you didn't know Michael Williams at all?

MD: No.

JC: All right. I think that covers it. Thanks for your time.

MD: You're welcome.

Professional Services Center • 2130 Topanga Creek Boulevard • Cummington, VA • 22769-8990
Office: (927) ███ • Local Pager: (927) ███

Josh and Heather in the Montgomery College edit room.

BUCHANAN'S
PRIVATE INVESTIGATIVE AGENCY, INC.
Serving Since 1940

This Report Constitutes Confidential Work Product and May Further Constitute Work Product of the Nature of an Attorney-Client Privilege

February 27, 1996
Re: BPIA #94-117

Transcript of Tape 94-117-61

Jennifer Colton: For the record, can you state your name?

Summer Leonard: Summer Leonard—I'm Joshua's mother.

JC: And you consent to the taping and transcription of this interview, Mrs. Leonard?

SL: I do.

JC: I want to thank you for agreeing to talk with me.

SL: Oh, Jacob would be very upset if he knew, but Angie's been so good to us . . . when she asked me to help out, I just couldn't say no.

JC: Well, I certainly appreciate it.

SL: I'm just not sure what I could tell you that I haven't already told the police.

JC: Sometimes a fresh perspective on things can help.

SL: All right. Ask your questions.

JC: Can you tell me a little bit about yourself and your husband, Mrs. Leonard? How long have your lived in this part of the country?

SL: Oh, I'm from around here. Jacob's family is from Richmond.

JC: What does your husband do?

SL: He's an insurance agent for GlobalMark. He works up in Frederick.

JC: How did Josh seem that week before the filming? Preoccupied, sad, happy . . .

SL: Oh, happy I would say. He was looking forward to making their movie.

JC: Go on.

SL: He just thought it was a very good idea Heather had.

JC: Were the two of them very close?

SL: No, not that I know of. I mean, they were friends from school, and she was over a few times to talk about the film, but other than that, I don't think they had much in common. Josh had a girlfriend at the time. They were pretty much living together, at her place.

JC: Who was she?

SL: A girl named Lisa Toller.

JC: Does she still live in the area?

SL: Oh yes. I saw her with her parents at the movies in Frederick last week.

JC: I'll get her number from you later, if that's all right.

SL: You know, I just remembered something about that week. Josh and Lisa were having a fight, I think.

JC: What makes you say that?

SL: Oh, my goodness, they were over here for dinner, and they didn't say ten words to each other. And later on, when they were up in his room, I could hear Josh raising his voice to her.

JC: Was that unusual? Did they fight a lot?

SL: No, not that I know of. Oh dear.

JC: What's the matter?

SL: That sounds like Jacob's car.

Professional Services Center • 2130 Topanga Creek Boulevard • Cummington, VA • 22769-8990
Office: (927) [redacted] • Local Pager: (927) [redacted]

Josh and his mother, Summer, during a vacation at the beach.

BUCHANAN'S
PRIVATE INVESTIGATIVE AGENCY, INC.
Serving Since 1940

This Report Constitutes Confidential Work Product and May Further Constitute Work Product of the Nature of an Attorney-Client Privilege

February 27, 1996
Re: BPIA #94-117

Transcript of Tape 94-117-69

Jennifer Colton: For the record, can you state your name?

Lisa Toller: Lisa Toller.

JC: And you consent to the taping and transcription of this interview?

LT: Yes, I do.

JC: Good. I want to ask you some questions about Joshua Leonard.

LT: Yeah, go on. My break is only ten minutes, though.

JC: I'll make this quick. First of all, do you have any idea who might have been involved in Josh's disappearance?

LT: No. Josh was friends with just about everybody.

JC: Can you think back to that week before his disappearance? Did he seem different to you at all?

LT: Oh. That was a horrible week.

JC: Why?

LT: Well . . . we were breaking up.

JC: Go on.

LT: See, he was just way too into the film thing he was doing, and I just didn't get it at all. Not even a little. Didn't want to talk about it, because that's the way I am—if something doesn't interest me or I think something's lame, I'm going to come right out and say it.

JC: That must have been hard.

LT: Well, it was awhile ago, honestly. I still think about Josh, but you know, I really really am sorry for him more than anything.

JC: Besides the film, did Josh have anything else on his mind that week? Anybody that he talked to you about?

LT: Yeah, that witch the film was about.

JC: The Blair Witch.

LT: The Blair Witch, yeah. He took a whole bunch of books out from the library on that Witch. He bought a notebook, and started writing stuff down in it all the time. He kept saying how "Heather" would appreciate it.

JC: You haven't seen that notebook recently, have you?

LT: No. I'm sure he took it with him to do the shoot.

JC: Did you know Mike Williams?

LT: I met him a couple of times. He was too much of a party animal for me, you know? I mean, that guy was always pounding brews.

JC: You didn't know him well, then?

LT: No.

JC: All right. Thank you, Lisa.

Professional Services Center • 2130 Topanga Creek Boulevard • Cummington, VA • 22769-8990
Office: (927) • Local Pager: (927)

Lisa Toller today.

MICHAEL WILLIAMS

The biographical sketch of himself Michael Williams composed to accompany Heather's thesis project.

At the age of 5, Mike won first prize in kindergarten for the best drawing of a fish. Since then he has won absolutely nothing except for "Least Likely to Succeed" in his graduating year of high school.

At 19 years old, he decided to head to St. Petersburg, FL, to work on a fishing boat called "The Old Kensico." Three months later he was back living at home.

He had also taken two courses in sound mixing and editing for film which is where he met Joshua Leonard. In October 1994, Josh called and asked him if he would like to join himself and Heather Donahue in shooting Heather's senior thesis project about the local legend of the Blair Witch. Mike accepted the job because he knew he could learn a lot from Josh and the experience.

BUCHANAN'S
PRIVATE INVESTIGATIVE AGENCY, INC.
Serving Since 1940

This Report Constitutes Confidential Work Product and May Further Constitute Work Product of the Nature of an Attorney-Client Privilege

March 1, 1996
Re: BPIA #94-117

Transcript of Tape 94-117-85

Jennifer Colton: For the record, can you state your name?

Cecilia DeCassan: Cecilia DeCassan.

JC: And you consent to the taping and transcription of this interview, Mrs. DeCassan?

CD: Yes, I do.

JC: You're good friends with the Williams family, is that right?

CD: Oh, yes. Our families have always been very close. I went to school with Maureen and all the Brody children when we were little.

JC: And you knew Michael?

CD: Yes. We've known Mike since he was born.

JC: And Tom, too?

CD: All the children. The whole family used to come down from New York during the summer and spend a couple weeks with us.

JC: What do you think happened to Michael?

CD: I don't like to think about that. It's just too horrible. That film they showed us . . .

JC: You think that's real?

CD: Of course it's real!

JC: Some people say the students faked the footage, that they faked their own disappearance.

CD: For an entire year and a half? You think they'd put their families through that? I don't know about those other kids, but not Michael. He would never, ever do that to his family.

JC: Michael was close to his family, huh?

CD: Yes. Well, I expect there was some tension—he was at that stage in a young man's life when you have to make your way out in the world—but I know there was a powerful love there.

JC: I did hear there was tension between Mike and his father.

CD: Young lady, I don't think I've ever known of a family where there was no tension between a father and the eldest son.

JC: What do you think happened to him?

CD: Something horrible got them in the woods.

JC: You're talking about the Blair Witch?

CD: I think there's some truth to that. I don't know what to call it—but everybody around here knows not to go fooling around out there. That's what the film shows—all those stick figures, and those rock piles. How does Ron Cravens explain that?

JC: Sheriff Cravens believes that proves the footage is a hoax.

CD: Oh, for pity's sake.

Professional Services Center • 2130 Topanga Creek Boulevard • Cummington, VA • 22769-8990
Office: (927) ███ • Local Pager: (927) ███

Cecilia DeCassan

BUCHANAN'S
PRIVATE INVESTIGATIVE AGENCY, INC.
Serving Since 1940

This Report Constitutes Confidential Work Product and May Further Constitute Work Product of the Nature of an Attorney-Client Privilege

March 1, 1996
Re: BPIA #94-117

Transcript of Tape 94-117-88 (continued)

Jennifer Colton: You were close to your brother, Mike, isn't that right Tom?

Tom Williams: Yes.

JC: What was his state of mind that week before the shoot?

TW: Well, I mean we were close but I didn't talk to him every day. We were both in school, living away from home—we didn't get to talk all that much.

JC: When you did talk, what did you talk about?

TW: I don't know. Sports. We both liked the Cowboys. Girls. Sometimes about his job.

JC: What about his job?

TW: Just that he liked it, you know. He wanted to be a recording engineer, get to tour with the rock bands, that kind of thing. He'd spent the summer doing some of the Lollapalooza dates. He was really psyched about that.

JC: Do you recall speaking with him the week before the film shoot?

TW: No, I don't.

JC: Was there anything bothering Mike in general?

TW: Just my dad. The two of them did not get along.

JC: What was the problem?

TW: It was just that father/son thing, you know. [laughter] I guess I'm not being too helpful.

JC: No, don't worry about it.

TW: Have you found any clues? Anything the police might have missed?

JC: We're still talking to people—but yes, there's a lot of things we've found that we can't explain.

TW: Not that Blair Witch crap, I hope?

JC: You don't believe in that legend, I take it?

TW: Oh come on. That's like the local Loch Ness monster.

JC: Some people take it pretty seriously. They even think the footage proves it exists.

TW: Oh, who? Like Mrs. DeCassan?

JC: Yes I spoke with her.

TW: Don't mention her to my dad—if you talk to him. That's all I can say.

JC: Why?

TW: Because he doesn't believe for a second that it was anything but some sick twisted bastard who killed my brother. And neither do I.

JC: All right.

TW: Mrs. DeCassan, Jesus. . . . would you believe that woman has never ever been into the Black Hills? Not even once?

JC: She seems pretty scared of the place.

TW: See? Is that crazy, or what? It's a bunch of trees, for Christ sakes.

Professional Services Center • 2130 Topanga Creek Boulevard • Cummington, VA • 22769-8990
Office: (927) ████ • Local Pager: (927) ████

Mike's brother, Tom Williams

BUCHANAN'S

PRIVATE INVESTIGATIVE AGENCY, INC.

Serving Since 1940

This Report Constitutes Confidential Work Product and May Further Constitute Work Product of the Nature of an Attorney-Client Privilege

March 1, 1996
Re: BPIA #94-117

Transcript of Tape 94-117-94

Jennifer Colton: Could you state your name for the record?

Jennifer Minor: Jennifer Minor.

JC: And you consent to the taping and transcription of this interview, Jennifer?

JM: I do.

JC: You were Mike Williams's girlfriend at the time of his disappearance?

JM: Yes.

JC: What can you tell me about Mike's state of mind that week before the film shoot?

JM: Well, he was pretty fried. The weekend before, he did this big concert for his job down in Baltimore, and I remember him cutting class on Monday. He didn't even get out of bed until like four in the afternoon.

JC: Was there anything bothering him? Anything at all you can remember?

JM: No. Well, except for getting all the equipment together, once Josh called him about the shoot.

JC: What do you mean?

JM: Michael didn't even know about the film until that week. This other girl who was a friend of Heather's was going to do sound, and at the last minute she got sick. Josh called Michael, and that's how he got on it.

JC: Did you ever hear him talk about the Blair Witch?

JM: No. I never even heard of the Blair Witch until this whole thing started, and I think it's creepy.

JC: You don't believe in it?

JM: No.

JC: Did Mike?

JM: I have no idea. God, it's funny to talk about him like this. I can't believe it's been like two years already he's gone.

JC: That's a nice picture of the two of you.

JM: Thanks.

JC: When was it taken?

JM: Oh, a few summers ago. My friend Liz Richardson took this when a bunch of us were at some local Chinese dump Mike liked—the Shanghai or something like that.

JC: Let's talk about Mike's friends for a second. Who was he close to?

JM: Oh, he hung out with everybody. Guys from his job, guys from school, me and my girlfriends—Mike liked to have fun. He liked everybody.

JC: Did he have any enemies?

JM: Not that I know of. Michael was just a sweet guy.

JC: All right. Thank you, Jennifer.

Professional Services Center • 2130 Topanga Creek Boulevard • Cummington, VA • 22769-8990
Office: (927) ████ • Local Pager: (927) ████

BUCHANAN'S

PRIVATE INVESTIGATIVE AGENCY, INC.

Serving Since 1940

This Report Constitutes Confidential Work Product and May Further Constitute Work Product of the Nature of an Attorney-Client Privilege

March 12, 1996
Re: BPIA #94-117

TO: Buck Buchanan

FROM: Jennifer Colton

RE: INTERVIEW TAPES

Accompanying this memo, please find a package containing forty microcassettes and transcripts of same.

To my eyes (and ears), there's not a lot to go on here: the DiGrassi lead seemed to be the strongest one we had. I'm sorry that didn't pan out.

I see three areas of focus for our continuing investigation:

1) Jim Donahue's background.

2) Continued archival research into state and national offender databases.

3) Expanding the search area to surrounding similarly wooded state parks. There are plenty of them in the area. See Tape 85: Mrs. DeCassan makes the same point you did.

I am available if you need me.

—JC

Professional Services Center • 2130 Topanga Creek Boulevard • Cummington, VA • 22769-8990

Office: (927) • Local Pager: (927)

March 21, 1996

Dear Buck,

Don't worry about Jim and I getting discouraged. It is disheartening at times when you look at how much work has been put into this case, and how relatively little information has emerged. But, we are not giving up.

Along those lines, we've dismissed Ken Reed as our attorney, and plan to hire one of Jim's friends from New York to pursue recovery of the footage.

I feel kind of strange bringing this up in a letter, but I think I'd feel even stranger bringing it up in a conversation. This whole Blair Witch business. I've been over Heather's journal now so many times I think I could

recite it by heart, and she clearly believed she was going to find something out there. I guess she was right.

Do you believe in the Blair Witch? I don't think I do... but I do want to try fighting fire with fire.

I read about all these police investigations where they bring in a psychic, or a mystic, or a what-have-you all the time. I wonder if you've had experience with this kind of person yourself. Would it be possible to get in touch with one?

As always, Jim and I appreciate everything you are doing.

Sincerely,

Angela Donahue

BUCHANAN'S
PRIVATE INVESTIGATIVE AGENCY, INC.
Serving Since 1940

March 26, 1996

Angela Donahue

Dear Angela:

I appreciate your continued persistence. I must admit to a little frustration—a lot of the ground we're going over now seems to have been covered by the police already.

But as I told you last week, the interviews gave us a few new areas to poke around in. I've sent one investigator to Washington, another's doing some interviews in New York, and I'll be doing a little more digging right here.

Regarding your question on the Blair Witch: I've actually had a researcher working on that aspect of the case for the last few days. I'm going to have him forward you a copy of everything he's found.

Now. About that psychic.

When I was in law enforcement, we used psychics from time-to-time. I have to say it never produced any results, and in my experience I never saw anything to make me believe in the supernatural or things like that. I won't say you're wasting your money if you want to go ahead and hire someone: I always think a fresh set of eyes can lend some perspective to an ongoing investigation.

I have someone in mind who I will contact, and tell about the case. She'll call you directly if she thinks she can help.

You know I wish you only the best of luck in finding Heather.

Sincerely,

Buck

C. D. Buchanan

Professional Services Center • 2130 Topanga Creek Boulevard • Cummington, VA • 22769-8990
Office: (927) ███ • Local Pager: (927) ███

AUTHOR'S NOTE:

So much of the preceding material does speak for itself that I find I have very little to add. The hard work, the blind alleys, the frustration—all are evident in the interviews and reports herein. What wasn't as clear to me on my first read of this material was how strongly it evoked the presence of the three missing students.

Buck and his team of investigators surely felt the same familiarity at this point in the investigation: they had all learned intimate details of Heather's, Josh's, and Mike's lives. Yet for all their efforts, they'd found nothing relevant to the case on hand. Their methods—in fact, their entire rational, scientific approach to the students' disappearance—produced no leads.

Angela Donahue was right. It was time to try another approach.

THE BLAIR WITCH

A timeline of those events most commonly considered part of the Blair Witch Legend.

THE LEGEND OF THE BLAIR WITCH

FEBRUARY 1785 Several children accuse Elly Kedward of luring them into her home to draw blood from them. Kedward is found guilty of witchcraft, banished from the village during a particularly harsh winter, and presumed dead.

NOVEMBER 1786 By midwinter all of Kedward's accusers, along with half the town's children, vanish. Fearing a curse, the townspeople flee Blair and vow never to utter Elly Kedward's name again.

1809 *The Blair Witch Cult* is published. This rare book, commonly considered fiction, tells the tale of an entire town cursed by an outcast witch.

1824 Burkittsville is founded on the Blair site.

AUGUST 1825 Eleven witnesses testify to seeing a pale woman's hand reach up and pull ten-year-old Eileen Treacle into Tappy East Creek. Her body is never recovered. For thirteen days after the drowning, the creek is clogged with oily bundles of sticks. The water becomes unpotable and may have been related to the death of a local who routinely used the creek's water for drinking.

MARCH 1886 Eight-year-old Robin Weaver is reported missing and search parties are dispatched. Although Weaver returns, one of the search parties does not. Their bodies are found weeks later at Coffin Rock, tied together at the arms and legs and completely disemboweled.

NOVEMBER 1940–MAY 1941 Starting with Emily Hollands, a total of seven children are abducted from the area surrounding Burkittsville, Maryland.

MAY 1941 An old hermit named Rustin Parr walks into a local market and tells the people there that he is "finally finished." After police hike for four hours to his secluded house in the woods, they find the bodies of seven missing children in the cellar. Each child has been ritualistically murdered and disemboweled. Parr admits to the killings, telling authorities a voice in his head—"an old woman"—commanded his actions. He is quickly convicted and hanged.

BUCHANAN'S
PRIVATE INVESTIGATIVE AGENCY, INC.
Serving Since 1940

This Report Constitutes Confidential Work Product and May Further Constitute Work Product of the Nature of an Attorney-Client Privilege

April 4, 1996
Re: BPIA #94-117

TO: ANGELA DONAHUE
FROM: C. SONENBERG
RE: BLAIR WITCH MATERIAL

As requested by Investigator Buchanan . . .

Herewith, copies of everything I could find on the Blair Witch Legend. It's very much an oral piece of history: a lot of people have heard of it, but there's virtually nothing written down anywhere.

Note that I've only attached partial transcripts of some of my interviews: should you desire more information, let me know, and I'll pass along the unedited material.

I hope you and your husband are well.

Professional Services Center • 2130 Topanga Creek Boulevard • Cummington, VA • 22769-8990
Office: (927) ████ • Local Pager: (927) ████

As part of his research into the Blair Witch Legend, Sonenberg spoke at length with noted folklore expert Professor Charles Moorehouse at Hampshire College.

BUCHANAN'S

PRIVATE INVESTIGATIVE AGENCY, INC.

Serving Since 1940

This Report Constitutes Confidential Work Product and May Further Constitute Work Product of the Nature of an Attorney-Client Privilege

March 28, 1996

Re: BPIA #94-117

Transcript of Tape 94-117-122 (continued)

Charles Moorehouse: The interesting thing about the Blair Witch is that it's one of the few American myths that virtually spans the history of this country. The legend goes all the way back to the late 1780s.

Carlos Sonenberg: That's about the time of the Bell Witch in Memphis, isn't it?

CM: The Bell Witch is Adams, Tennessee, actually. But you're right—the two are roughly contemporary. The Blair Witch is the far more interesting legend, though, because there are events associated with it occurring right through to modern times.

CS: You're talking about Rustin Parr?

CM: No. It's my belief that what Parr did should not be considered part of the mythos. In fact, I've heard it suggested that he killed those children just to become part of the legend. I was referring to the Robin Weaver story.

CS: I have that here somewhere. . . . [rustling paper] That's the one where the search party doesn't come back.

CM: That's right. What makes that particularly interesting are the contemporary newspaper accounts. A bit florid, but still—the persistence in assigning a supernatural explanation to the extraordinary is so typical. It's the Salem Witch Trials all over again. If you can't find an explanation for it, it must be the devil's work.

CS: What strikes me is the cyclical nature of the legend. A new incident every fifty years, always involving children.

CM: Yes.

CS: This time, it's the missing Montgomery College film students.

CM: I suppose.

CS: You don't sound like a believer, Professor.

CM: Not in an old woman who lives out in the woods and eats little children, no.

CS: What do you think happened to the film students?

CM: I really don't know.

CS: In the article you wrote for *Paranormal*, you pointed to the writing seen briefly on the house walls, during the final few minutes of footage. You were of the opinion that if you had a copy of that footage to study closely, that script could be deciphered.

[CONTINUED]

Professional Services Center • 2130 Topanga Creek Boulevard • Cummington, VA • 22769-8990
Office: (927) ████ • Local Pager: (927) ████

From the mythology and folklore collection of Theo Lotz.

Following pages, a selection of the more interesting documents Sonenberg uncovered in his research. Below, an early reference to the Black Hills, from *American Folklore Before the Pioneers* by Alan Stansfield. Published 1899 by H. Roberts and Sons.

large stretches of the Appalachians were merely hunting lands[3]. There were also territories that remained unsettled for other reasons.

One of the most interesting such territories is the Black Hills forest, which we first find mention of in the correspondence of Martin Pheypo, a cousin of Cecil Calvert, the second Lord Baltimore and the founder of Maryland. In 1632, Pheypo led a party of twelve men into the Appalachians. They planned to establish a trading post and subsequently, a garrison to guard the colony's western flank.

Along the way, they encountered unexpected difficulties, and Pheypo was forced to return to Baltimore having failed to accomplish his mission. He later wrote to Calvert:

14th June
Honorable Cousin:

Yours of the 7th this instant received. I am sorry that my extraordinary occasions will not permit me to be at the next Provincial Court, to be held in Maryland the 4th this next month. Because then, God willing, I intend to get my young son baptized, all the company and gossips being already invited. Your Lordship's presence will be missed.

You asked for details of our adventure, and it is my pleasure to provide them. Not because I am happy with our party's lack of accomplishment—I am not—but because I desire you to have all relevant details to inform your future judgements in this area.

Our journey west was accomplished without incident—we had the good fortune to have as our guide a Yaocomicoe brave of uncommon intelligence and character. We reached the Catocin, when the most extraordinary thing happened.

Upon seeing the foothills and forests before us, our guide—whose Indian name I shall not attempt to pronounce, but shall refer to by the good Christian name we gave him of Robert—refused to go further. Lacking in knowledge of the Yaocomicoe tongue, we were unable to comprehend his reasons, and were forced to insist on his continuance.

That evening, Robert attempted to drive off our horses, to prevent our further journey westward. Mr. Scott, who initially mistook him for an intruder, shot and killed the unfortunate savage.

Without the direction of our guide, we were left with little choice but to return east, to Baltimore.

It is my suggestion that future expeditions include both surveyors and soldiers. A Tristam Piernont, resident of your Lordship's colony, is known to me as a map-maker; for a commander, recusing myself, I think most highly of Colonel Nathan Blair.

Your compliant servant,
Martin Pheypo[4]

Robert's refusal to lead the party into the forests of what we now call the Black Hills was repeated on another occasion as well. A group of explorers striking out from the

Sonenberg's intensive research into the native history of the area came up with one other interesting anomaly: Many tribes settled the region, most notably the Nanticoke, who had actively traded with the Delaware and Susquehanna people to the north and the Powhatan to the south. Some tribes had even founded alliances with Algonquin and Iroquois-speaking nations farther away, adopting their forest-oriented culture. As they did, marine resources became far less important economically than were products gleaned from woodland plants and animals. Interestingly enough though, while many villages indeed flourished near what was later to become the town of Blair, there are no indigenous records of any kind that point to natives in or around the Black Hills Forest.

From the Burkittsville Historical Society, a reproduction of correspondence between Colonel Blair and his father back in England—the first known reference to the township of Blair, sent seven days before Nathan Blair succumbed to the illness of which he speaks.

(31)

30 August
Father --

A short note this time. I have received your letter of last June, and you should insure Jonathan that we will not run out of land here in the Colonies. No matter how many houses are built here in Blair, there will always be room for one more, which is to say, his.

Nathaniel

8 November
Father --

Can it truly be a year already that I have called this village home? It does not seem possible. And yet here we are, two score of us, eking our living from the land and protecting the western flank of Lord Calvert's colony. The French and their Indian lackeys seem reluctant to test our strength: God willing, this will remain the case, as I am attached to this countryside. Not, I assure you, simply because the village grown up around our garrison has become commonly known by my own name. Though I admit to some desire to have the Blair name live on in history, it is the people here who command my allegiance to this land.

Virginia is settling in; truly, she is a different person than the delicate girl you remember from Mayfair. I had shared your trepidation over her adjustment to life in the colonies, especially after the terrible events on the Honeycutt during her voyage here. You would be astonished to see the garden she has made here alongside our cabin. It is a treasure of spices and herbs: she has even found a leaf which makes a passable tea. A good thing: I have become ill these last two weeks, and have lost five stone. The tea settles my stomach, and allows me to both eat, and sleep.

News from home would be welcome: you and Jonathan are

Virginia Blair, circa 1630, artist unknown. After his death, Nathan Blair's wife virtually ran the burgeoning outpost. A rare example of a woman wielding power in Colonial America. Courtesy of the Mayfair Town Archives.

BUCHANAN'S
PRIVATE INVESTIGATIVE AGENCY, INC.
Serving Since 1940

This Report Constitutes Confidential Work Product and May Further Constitute Work Product of the Nature of an Attorney-Client Privilege

March 28, 1996
Re: BPIA #94-117
Transcript of Tape 94-117-122 (continued)

Charles Moorhouse: Witch hunts in Europe were responsible for the deaths of more than 200,000 people. It was the church, you see: their consolidation of power, their elimination of competing belief systems. Protestants, midwives, herbalists—

Charles Sonenberg: Not just old women, I gather.

CM: Oh, no. Men, young girls, political targets—whoever was on the wrong side of the church or the local authorities. Which is one of the reasons why the hysteria never really made its way across the Atlantic. People who came to the colonies were running away from the established power structure, looking for a fresh start. Though they could revert to their old fears under the right circumstances.

CS: Like the Salem Witch Trials.

CM: Salem, yes. Or a captain, experiencing a particularly difficult ocean crossing, might put the blame on one of his passengers—a woman, usually—who was obviously a witch in disguise. There are several examples in the literature of these "witches" being put to death at sea.

CS: So tell me how the Blair Witch legend starts.

CM: The Blair Witch legend starts with an old woman named Elly Kedward who was convicted in 1785 of drawing blood from several of the town's children to make "magic potions." The townspeople cast her out in the middle of winter, leaving her to wander and no doubt die in the wilderness. A few months later, the town's children begin disappearing. The parents blame it on Elly and abandon the town of Blair.

CS: Which eventually becomes Burkittsville.

CM: Exactly. Of course, a far more rational explanation for the children's disappearance is the presence of nearby Indian tribes. Nonetheless, by the end of the following year, the village of Blair is no more.

CS: What happens next?

CM: In the Blair Witch legend?

CS: Yes.

CM: The publication of a book called "The Blair Witch Cult," sometime around the turn of the century. That's when the term "The Blair Witch" first comes into play.

[CONTINUED]

Professional Services Center • 2130 Topanga Creek Boulevard • Cummington, VA • 22769-8990
Office: (927) ████ • Local Pager: (927) ████

In an eighteenth-century woodcut by local artisan Ethan Long, Elly Kedward is banished from the town of Blair, bound on a wheelbarrow. There are conflicting reports of the Elly Kedward story: the best of these is Cece Malvey's "Wood Witch Said," though I suggest the reader seek out some of the more modern abridgements than the laboriously drawn-out original.

A selection of woodcuts and depictions of witches and witchcraft.

BUCHANAN'S
PRIVATE INVESTIGATIVE AGENCY, INC.
Serving Since 1940

This Report Constitutes Confidential Work Product and May Further Constitute Work Product of the Nature of an Attorney-Client Privilege

March 28, 1996
Re: BPIA #94-117
Transcript of Tape 94-117-29

Carlos Sonenberg: Mr. Barnes?

Bill Barnes: Yes.

CS: This is Carlos Sonenberg. I spoke to you a couple days ago about the missing students?

BB: Oh yes. How are you, Mr. Sonenberg?

CS: Fine, thank you. Can I ask you a few more questions, specifically about the Blair Witch legend?

BB: Go right ahead. That's my job.

CS: Would you mind if I recorded this call?

BB: Well. . . . I suppose not.

CS: I wanted to follow up on something I saw in that tape you gave me—a book called *The Blair Witch Cult*?

BB: Oh, yes.

CS: Can you tell me about that?

BB: Well, a few months ago I could have done better than that. I could've shown it to you. Had a copy right here in Burkittsville. Then some muckety-mucks at the Maryland Historical Society decided it would do more good sitting in their research library than out here on display for everybody to see, and so they took it back from us.

CS: That sounds stupid.

BB: Hell, it is stupid, but try talking sense to a bunch of librarians.

CS: Yeah.

BB: What do you want to know about the book?

CS: What's it about?

BB: As near as anyone can figure—and again, the copy we have—the only copy I know of that exists—close to half the book is illegible because the paper's rotted away—it's a story about some of the things that went on in Blair, right after the time of Elly Kedward.

CS: What kind of stories?

BB: Oh all sorts of horrible things. Witches sacrificing children, witches changing into wolves, rats, and all sorts of other animals. A lot that's surely apocryphal . . . it starts off with the author explaining how witches first came to America, even, how there was a group of them on trial in England who escaped onto a ship, and then killed and took the place of some of the highborn women already on board. When they land, some go north to Salem, some go to the other colonies, like Maryland. . . .

CS: It's a history?

BB: Oh no, not really. Most of it focuses around the Elly Kedward legend, and around Blair. Sort of the cult that forms around Elly—around the Blair Witch. Some of the stuff that takes place in it, there are other sources verifying that these things actually happened.

[CONTINUED]

Professional Services Center • 2130 Topanga Creek Boulevard • Cummington, VA • 22769-8990

Office: (927) [redacted] • Local Pager: (927) [redacted]

The objects depicted here are claimed to have been used by the cult in conjunction with the book.

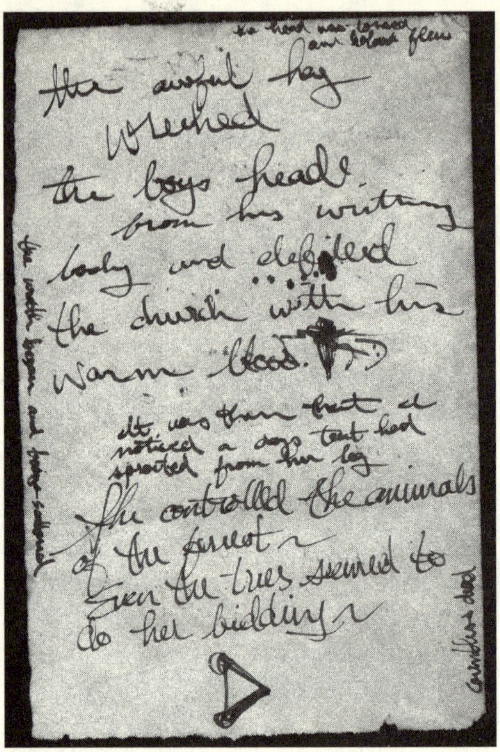

The Blair Witch Cult book is a collection of almost incoherent ramblings purporting to tell about the history of the Blair Witch, archaic rituals, and assorted witchcraft. Only one volume is known to exist.

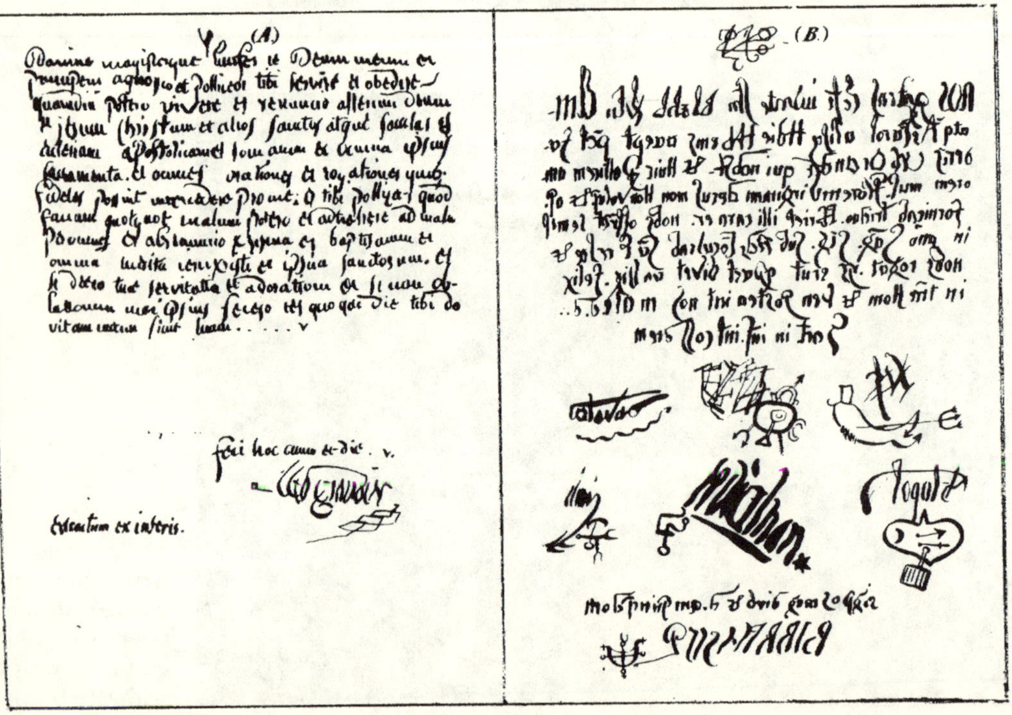

Blair becomes Burkittsville: below, a newspaper article outlining the founding of a new town by Peter Branwall Burkitt, a wealthy plantation owner from Baltimore. The story goes that a friend of Burkitt's was a railroad baron in Maryland, and while his men were working on the railroad he became lost in the woods and stumbled on the overgrown road leading to Blair. Knowing of Burkitt's desire to develop land, he tips his friend off. Both die in their beds, extremely wealthy men.

THE MARYLAND JOURNAL, AND THE BALTIMORE ADVERTISER.

Containing the FRESHEST ADVICES, both FOREIGN and DOMESTIC.

FRIDAY, AUGUST 20, 1823 [Vol. I.]

Baltimore, May 24.

Captain John Salter, of the brig Betsy, arrived, on the 7th instant, at Portsmouth, New-Hampshire, in 48 days from Dartmouth; England, informs, that there was a very hot press in most of the British ports, and that orders had been issued to double the militia; that about 25 sail of the line had sailed from Brest, a variety of conjectures were formed of their destination, among which that they had gone to the West-Indies.

PROGRESS OF THE WAR.

MATAMORAS TAKEN WITHOUT OPPOSITION.

SMITH'S Ferry, on Susquehanna. On this plantation there are a good square log dwelling-house, with three rooms on a floor, an excellent spring and spring-house near the door, a double barn, and stables, a good young apple and peach orchard, with seven acres of watered meadow, and more may easily be made. The whole is in good repair, and a good title will be given, by

December 13, 1791. JOHN PATTERSON.

THIS FASHIONABLE AND POPULAR PLACE OF RESORT

A GRAND BALL

Shooting Galleries,

Keefer & Snoke, Dealers in Choice Family Flour and Mill Feed.

We have lately refitted our room and purchased a full assortment of groceries and provisions, which we will sell as cheap as the cheapest. To satisfy yourselves give us a call and examine our goods.

Goods delivered free to all parts of the city. We also keep a full line of the best brands of cigars and tobaccos. We would not forget to tender our thanks to the citizens of Marion and vicinity for your past favors, and would still be thankful for a share of your patronage. Remember our room, Miller's Block, one door north of Kerr House, Marion, O. 138m3

A maniac in Natick, Mass., caught a glimpse through a window of a woman in her night clothes, and thought she was an angel. This was complimentary to the beauty, but dangerous to her life, for he fired at her with a pistol to find out whether she really wasn't human. The bullet grazed her head.

A grass fire overtook a man in San Bernardino, Cal., and he had barely time to reach a creek. He rolled over and over in the shallow water, scorched by the flames that swept overhead, and was almost smothered. The terrible heat lasted only a few seconds, but sufficiently long to burn off his hair and char his clothing.

A Harrisburg, Pa., jeweller says that neither he nor one of his workmen uses tobacco, and both can handle any polished tool in the shop and lay it aside unwiped without injury. The other workmen use tobacco habitually, and if they neglect to wipe polished tools after using them rust spots will soon invariably appear.

Persons who send original jokes to the Mansfield (Ind.) Monitor are requested to sign their real names, not necessarily for publication, but in order that they may be added to the statistics of the Lunatic Asylum.

OLYMPIC (FORMERLY) Gilbert's Melodeon

N E CORNER CLAY AND KEARNY STREETS.

GREAT COMEDY NIGHT

First Appearance of JIMMY MURPHY

SENORITA MARIA AND LITTLE LULU

Wednesday Evening, May 24

A NEW WALK AROUND—Hunting ob de Co

Mrs. BLOOD, Fashionable Milliner,

Fashionable Millinery Goods

Constantly on hand and Made to Order, in the LATEST STYLE

Mrs. M. D. GAGE, CLOAK AND DRESS MAKER,

Opera Season.

Vanilla, Strawberry and Lemon ICE CREAM WITH STRAWBERRIES,

PETER JOB'S,

HAGAN & HARRIS,

SALE YARD 423 PACIFIC STREET,

BETWEEN SANSOME & MONTGOMERY,

BUYING AND SELLING STOCK

Bradley & Rulofson

CELEBRATED Photograph Gallery

CORNER SACRAMENTO AND MONTGOMERY,

Groceries!

FOR ALL KINDS OF

Groceries, Queensware,

Moralist, No. XIV.

"And Sampson said unto his father, get her for me; for she pleaseth me."

WHILE our champion was free from the nuptial tie, he journied to Timnah, where he was enamored by the beautiful appearance of a Philistine girl. All the remonstrances of his discerning parents could not persuade him to abandon his intentions, because, said he, "she pleaseth me."

O precipitate man! How did she please you, when folded in the arms of your friend! How, when she declared the interpretation of your riddle to the Philistines! Did she thereby excite your esteem, and render the after period of your life more pleasant and agreeable? If so, let posterity follow the example; listen to the syren song of wanton inspiration, and bask in the sunshine of voluptuous ease and indulgence. If not, let them pursue a different course. The alluring smiles of the harlot, will, assuredly be like vinegar to the teeth, or gall to the palate—Though she says, "I have perfumed my bed with myrrh, aloes and cinnamon," believe her not, neither listen at all to her voice, 'for her house is the way to hell, going down to the chambers of death.'

HOTEL ARRIVALS.

KERR HOUSE.

S H Royce Monticello N Y
B Fancett Cleveland
Wm Scott Buffalo
S E Browne Columbus
E Illinsworth N Y
L D Austin Toledo
W S Hase Columbus
T S Henry Cleveland
J H Henry do
Chas S S Lennox N Y
W A Murray Cleveland
E Moyer Nevada
Chas Longstreet N Y
J W White Johnstown
Peter Copeland do
James A Mease Cleveland
Horace Gask Columbus
Wm Parry Urbana
Frank McCulloch Philadelphia
Geo W Dove N Y
J H Horton Buffalo
J F Filler Cincinnati
J K Stauffer Annandale N Y

Land Purchase

Baltimore land baron Peter Branwell Burkitt has purchased a substantial Tract of land at the site of Maryland's newest railroad. Mr. Burkitt surveyed the land earlier this year and found it to be rich in a limestone of superior quality. He expressed a strong desire to take advantage of the new railroad which has access to Baltimore and Washington. Mr. Burkitt also claims that there is what appears to be a previous settlement although nothing would support his endorsement. Perhaps it is an ancient settlement? The plot consists of three thousand acres bounded on the east by a river and on the north side by the railroad. Mr. Burkitt has begun plans for a township which he states "will one day rival our great cities of Baltimore and Philadelphia."

SPICER'S Pocket Companion.

AND THE YOUNG LADY'S ACCIDENCE.

FOR SALE BY James Springer.

A Bargain.

GIDEON CORNELL.

FOR SALE, BY EPHRAIM M. FAIR

50 barrels Superfine Flour, fresh from Albertson's Mills, Long-Island, 45000 Lumber, and a few Kegs Virginia manufactured Tobacco

FOR SALE, BY ISAAC TREBY, 40 barrels Mess PORK

Wanted Immediately A QUANTITY OF Old Copper and Brass

Ten Dollars Reward.

JOSEPH DURR,

AROMATIC PASTE

ISAAC THOMPSON

BUCHANAN'S
PRIVATE INVESTIGATIVE AGENCY, INC.
Serving Since 1940

This Report Constitutes Confidential Work Product and May Further Constitute Work Product of the Nature of an Attorney-Client Privilege

March 28, 1996
Re: BPIA #94-117
Transcript of Tape 94-117-122 (continued)

Charles Moorehouse: The next incident occurs in 1825, when a young girl named Eileen Treacle drowns in a creek near Burkittsville. Witnesses claim to see an arm reach up out of the water and pull her under. They never found the body, even though the creek was only two feet deep.

Carlos Sonenberg: You can drown in an inch of water, if you land in the water right.

CM: My point exactly—the logical explanation for what happened in this instance is simply that. The girl falls somehow, is carried downstream, and disappears.

CS: Doesn't sound so mystical.

CM: It's not. It's what happens afterwards that paints this incident as part of the Blair Witch Legend. For the next few weeks, the creek water becomes fouled and unuseable.

CS: Unuseable? How?

CM: Poisoned, I believe. There's actually some contemporary documentation of this occurrence—

CS: I'd be interested in seeing that.

CM: I'll see if I can get copies for you later. At any rate, the other thing that happens is that all these little bundles of sticks start washing up near the town—

CS: Bundles of sticks?

CM: Yes.

CS: Can I show you a picture of something?

CM: Yes.

CS: Hold on a minute, I left the folder in the car.

****

CS: What do you make of these?

CM: What is it—some kind of scarecrow?

CS: No. These are what was on the footage we found. What the students came across.

CM: Bundles of sticks.

CS: Exactly.

CM: Hmmm. That's very interesting.

CS: What do you think? Are they connected?

CM: They could be, yes. . . .

CS: All right. How about these?

CM: Also on the students' footage?

CS: Yes.

CM: A pile of stones like this—the first thing I think of is some kind of burial cairn. But that doesn't make sense—that's an Old World custom. I suppose it could be a carryover from Europe . . . could indicate a landmark of some kind too, I suppose.

CS: That doesn't sound right. The students found three of these piles outside their tent one morning.

CM: Three students, three piles. That makes sense. Three graves? It seems to me what you have here is someone taking advantage of the legend to scare these kids.

CS: Maybe to do more than scare them.

[CONTINUED]

Professional Services Center • 2130 Topanga Creek Boulevard • Cummington, VA • 22769-8990
Office: (927) ████ • Local Pager: (927) ████

Contemporary sources referencing the Eileen Treacle incident.

Journal entry of Lloyd Whellons, May 5, 1877 (relating incidents of her childhood)

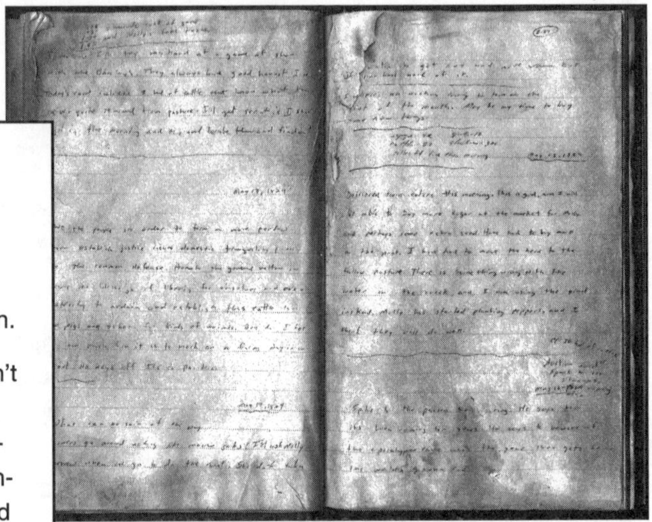

1828 was one of the worst years I remember. Illness swept my town, and no family was left unscathed. Papa died that year, and we were left to manage the crops on our own.

The harvest was bad, but we weren't the only ones suffering. Indians razed a town to the east of us, murdering every soul living there. A panther went into a woman's house and ate her child right out of the crib, and a little girl was drowned, and the town claimed the devil himself had pulled her down into the water.

Mid-nineteenth-century illustration of the Eileen Treacle incident.

BURKITTSVILLE BULLETIN

VOL. 5 BURKITTSVILLE, MARYLAND AUGUST 14, 1825

THE INAUGURATION CROWD

WASHINGTON FILLING UP WITH VISITORS.

ALL THE HOTELS OVERFLOWING - MANY DISTINGUISHED MEN ON HAND - PREPARING FOR THE GREAT PROCESSION.

Washington, March 1 - Since early this morning every railway train which has reached Washington from any direction has come crowded with visitors to the capital, and the inauguration rush is now well under way. Despite the most disagreeable, "sticky" weather, marked at frequent intervals with drizzling rain, many hundreds of strangers have promenaded the streets and avenues as if anxious to lose no time in looking about the city. The lobbies of all the principal hotels have been overflowing all day with visitors seeking rooms engaged by them long ago and with others foolish enough to suppose that they could find hotel accommodation engaged three days before the inauguration. While the hotel rooms are all taken, and have been for some time, there are still unengaged quarters for several thousand persons in boarding houses throughout the city, and those who have applied unsuccessfully at hotels have had little difficulty in securing rooms elsewhere. Members of the Public Comfort Committee were stationed at each of the railway stations at 6 o'clock this morning, and will remain on duty there until Wednesday noon. They are provided with lists of boarding houses and rates, and can assign quarters to all who desire them. For the last two weeks, this committee has provided for from 50 to 60 private parties every day, and it still has on its books rooms for over 40,000 persons. The first day's work of the committee at the stations has been a busy one. The stations have been thronged all day with new arrivals and the railroad companies have prepared for a big traffic. The Baltimore and Ohio Company has increased its facilities for handling passengers by laying extra tracks into the city and by arranging for the running of many extra trains from all points, and it is bring in great crowds of people by every train.

The hundreds of military and civic organizations from all over the United States which are to take part in the great inauguration parade will begin to arrive tomorrow, and the committees which are to look after their comfort are ready for a busy time. Many will be mot by local organizations, who will escort them to their quarters, and all will find some one on hand to see that they do not get lost in the streets. The Pennsylvania militia, who are remembered by all who saw the parade four years ago, are expected early tomorrow evening. An hour or two later, Tammany's 1,000 braves are expected. They will find the Jackson Democratic Association ready to receive them with artillery salutes and fireworks and to march with them to the furniture warehouse in which they are to lodge. The great rush of visiting organizations, however, will be on Tuesday. Arrangements for the procession have been made.

MURPHY'S SLAYERS CONVICTED

TWO OF THEM FOUND GUILTY OF MURDER AND THE OTHER OF MANSLAUGHTER.

New Orleans, March 1. - The famous Ford murder trial came to an end late last night, the jury bringing in a verdict of guilty of murder against
Patrick Ford and John
manslaughter against
Ford, W. E. Caulfiel
Buckley. This has
exciting murder trial
witnessed since the w
was a lending Demo
and Recorder of the
the city. He has a qu
Murphy, likewise a De
a sporting man, amate
Deputy Workhouse K
Ford, talking with h
Patrick and three polic
court, waited in ambu
upon Murphy while un
duty in charge of a ga
laborers. All were
attacked him, but Mu
Ford, the testimony s
three fatal shots. In
the killing, leading city
of Ford, organized s
intimidation of w
although the killing w
scores of people, hard
first be found to test
Jury spent 30 days
case. The accused men were brought to trial on Jan. 27, and the trial occupied 10 days. After the trial

DESTRUCTIVE FIRE IN ALBANY

A LARGE FREIGHT HOUSE BURNED - AND CHEMICAL WORKS MUCH DAMAGED

ALBANY, March 1. Albany way visited today by one of the most destructive and threatening fires in many years. Originating in the eastern end of the huge frame freight house of the Albany and Susquehanna Railroad Company, used also by the West Shore Company, the flames spread with great rapidity, and at one time it was feared that the whole southern portion of the city would be destroyed. The firemen worked admirably under many disadvantages, the water mains not being large enough to furnish the requisite supply of water. The dying out of a strong south wind about noon and the setting in of a heavy rain soon after undoubtedly saved very much property from destruction. Master Mechanic Blackwell, of the Deleware and Hudson, thought the company's loss would be in the neighborhood of $50,000. About 40 cars were damaged. The West Showe Company owned most of the freight, and the Delaware and Hudson Canal Company the greater number of the cars. The

CHILD DIES IN CREEK

A young child drowned yesterday in the shallow waters of Tappy East Creek. The Treacle Family is mourning the probable loss of their youngest child, Eileen, who is ten. The child's Body has not yet been found. The Treacle family had joined several other local families for our annual Wheat Harvest Picnic. Many people claim they heard a "raucous splashing" and then saw the child struggling from afar. No one was able to arrive quickly enough to save this young life. Please take time to offer your prayers to the Treacle family.

enough to save this young life, Please take time to offer your prayers to the Treacle family.

BUCHANAN'S

PRIVATE INVESTIGATIVE AGENCY, INC.

Serving Since 1940

This Report Constitutes Confidential Work Product and May Further Constitute Work Product of the Nature of an Attorney-Client Privilege

March 28, 1996

Re: BPIA #94-117

Transcript of Tape 94-117-29 (continued)

Carlos Sonenberg: So you actually knew Robin Weaver.

Bill Barnes: Oh, yes. She was an old woman by then, but she still lived out on Chilton Highway, in the same house her parents had raised her up in.

CS: Did she ever talk about it?

BB: Well, son, you have to understand that she was more than a little on the eccentric side. She talked about a lot of things and not very many of them made sense. So she never talked about the incident directly, no. As a matter of fact, now that I think about it, I don't think she ever talked at all about what happened to her in that time she spent out in the woods, even when she was younger. Never said a word about it—at least nothing that I ever heard of.

CS: Do you think she remembered it?

BB: I really don't know.

CS: Was she different after the incident? I guess that would be hard for you to say—you didn't know her before.

BB: That's true. But you know, there is one thing. I remember—I think it was right before she died, so it must have been 1943, 1944—yes, right in the middle of the war—I was just sitting on the steps of the general store with some friends of mine, gosh, I can't even recall who it was—and we were talking about how we should send someone who was really good at killing to take care of the Germans. And somebody—I think it might have been Luther Cravens, who was Sheriff Cravens's uncle, he was about my age—Luther said, "we should send them Rustin Parr." You know who Rustin Parr is, right?

CS: Yes. I know who Rustin Parr is.

BB: Well, then I said Rustin Parr wouldn't do no killing without those voices to guide him. And Miss Weaver—Robin Weaver—she walks by just at that moment, and she says, "Yeah, Jesus. Send the voices. I know those voices. Send them the voices."

CS: Huh.

BB: Yeah. What do you make of that?

[CONTINUED]

Professional Services Center • 2130 Topanga Creek Boulevard • Cummington, VA • 22769-8990

Office: (927) ████ • Local Pager: (927) ████

The gruesome fate of the first search party sent out to find Robin Weaver. This drawing, from *McClory's Illustrated*, shows one of the many differing accounts of how the men were found.

Robin Weaver as a young girl.

The second search party sent out to find Robin Weaver after her disappearance, photographed here at Coffin Rock.

A folk song from the late 1800s. "Tom Kane" in the third verse could be a corruption of "Tom Lang," who was one of the search party victims found bound and disemboweled.

Kind friends listen now to my terrible tale
Take this warning to heart lest you walk danger's trail
Bolt tight all your doors keep a light on the sill
And don't walk at night through the woods of Black Hills

Stay away from the heart of the forest my friend
Stay away lest you never see daylight again
'Neath the warm summer sun all is peaceful and still
But don't walk at night through the woods of Black Hills

Tom Kane was my husband so dear to my heart
We swore to ourselves that we never would part
We passed all our days in contentment until
He went for a walk in the woods of Black Hills

Stay away from the heart of the forest my friend
Keep your children from wandering hold to your men
When the moon blossoms full when the river is still
There's a darkness that waits in the woods of Black Hills

RUSTIN PARR

While Sonenberg was putting together his report on the legend of the Blair Witch, Buck Buchanan was busy trying to reconcile inconsistencies within the case as he saw them. The following conversation took place late in March, shortly before Deputy Hart left the Burkittsville Sheriff's Office.

BUCHANAN'S
PRIVATE INVESTIGATIVE AGENCY, INC.
Serving Since 1940

This Report Constitutes Confidential Work Product and May Further Constitute Work Product of the Nature of an Attorney-Client Privilege

March 28, 1996
Re: BPIA #94-117
Transcript of Tape 94-117-97

Buck Buchanan: I'm stating for the record that this conversation is being recorded for investigative purposes, with the understanding that it will be transcribed and a copy of that transcription provided to my client for her information. Is that your understanding?

Hank Hart: Yes, it is.

CDB: Would you please state your name.

HH: Hank Hart.

CDB: And your occupation?

HH: I'm a deputy of the Burkittsville Sheriff's Office [laughter]. For the next two weeks I am, anyway.

CDB: You wanted to talk to me about something.

HH: Yes, I did. I appreciate the way you handled yourself during all that craziness at the beginning of the year. I know Ron did too, even if he didn't come right out and say it.

CDB: Well, thank you. I appreciate how cooperative you were to myself and everybody working for Mrs. Donahue.

HH: Right.

CDB: What did you want to tell me?

HH: What I wanted to tell you . . . I don't even know how to . . . the best way to begin this. Hmmm. I guess I should start off by saying that Ron and me have been buddies since high school.

CDB: Ron is Sheriff Cravens?

HH: That's right. And I think I know him better than just about anybody else. Damn sight better than that woman he married, anyway. And Ron don't like it when the boat gets rocked.

CDB: Yeah. I picked that up.

[laughter]

HH: Yeah. I suppose you did. But listen, Ron is a straight shooter. He doesn't say anything he doesn't truly believe, from the bottom of his heart.

CDB: I appreciate that.

HH: In his mind, there's no way that footage is anything other than fake. Because there's no way that anyone is creeping through the woods outside of town, looking to kill people.

CDB: Okay.

HH: So that's the official position. But as for myself . . . listen, there's a lot of weird shit that's happened in that woods. Creepy stuff.

CDB: I've heard about some of it.

HH: You heard about Rustin Parr?

CDB: Yes, of course.

HH: Well, that's the thing that worries me. All that serial killer stuff—what I worry about, is that there's somebody out there doing these things again—

CDB: Like a copycat?

HH: A copycat, that's exactly it. And you know the FBI brought that up when they were here, but I couldn't really talk to them officially, because that would have sent Ron off the deep end.

CDB: I know that's something they looked into.

HH: Yeah, I know that too, but they sure as hell didn't tell me anything. Do they think there's some kind of serial killer up in the woods?

CDB: They're not acting like it, are they?

HH: No.

CDB: I have a friend, who used to be pretty high up in the agency, and he did a little sniffing around for me, and he told me they weren't treating this like anything but a missing persons case.

HH: Good, because . . . I mean, I've been sitting here, with this thing building up inside of me, and I thought you'd be a guy I could talk to about it, who might actually be able to do something.

CDB: Yeah. My friend could. Maybe.

HH: Okay. You should know first of all, that I think that footage is genuine. I think somebody was stalking those kids up there. I don't think they were faking it.

CDB: Neither do I.

HH: All the Feds felt that way, too. So what I want to show you is this [sound of papers shuffling]. This is a copy of the original police report from back in 1940, back when Rustin Parr killed those kids.

CDB: Uh-huh.

HH: And here [more paper shuffling] . . . this is the part that scared me. This is testimony from this kid who escaped from Parr, about how—

CDB: Wait a minute. A kid escaped? I didn't know about that.

HH: Yeah. Kyle Brody—little nine-year-old boy. And here . . . listen to this. This is what he told the police. "Then he said I had to stand in the corner. And he said I had to listen, but I couldn't watch. I had to stand facing the corner."

CDB: Jesus.

HH: Yeah. That's the same way the Williams boy was standing in the footage.

CDB: That's something.

HH: I think so. I hope not, but . . . it could be.

CDB: Can I get a copy of that? I'll put an associate of mine on this right away.

HH: Yeah. These are all for you. Like I said, I hope you can do something with the information.

CDB: I do too. I appreciate you coming out here and talking like this, Hank. I know Mrs. Donahue does as well.

HH: Hell, it's no problem. Least thing I could do. I feel terrible about what happened to their kids, and I wish we could have found out a little more for them.

CDB: Is that all you wanted to say?

HH: I think so.

Professional Services Center • 2130 Topanga Creek Boulevard • Cummington, VA • 22769-8990
Office: (927) ████ • Local Pager: (927) ████

BUCHANAN'S
PRIVATE INVESTIGATIVE AGENCY, INC.
Serving Since 1940

This Report Constitutes Confidential Work Product and May Further Constitute Work Product of the Nature of an Attorney-Client Privilege

March 28, 1996
Re: BPIA #94-117

TO: Buck Buchanan
FROM: Carlos Sonenberg
RE: RUSTIN PARR

Thanks for the heads-up about Brody. Here's the other material I got on Rustin Parr: I didn't send any of this material to Mrs. Donahue. Reason number one: I agree with what Professor Moorehouse said—it doesn't really fit in with the other "Blair Witch" episodes. It's too recent, too graphic, and doesn't add anything to those bits of the legend she's concerned with, in my opinion. If you feel differently, well then—obviously—send her whatever you please.

Reason number two. . . .

Well, take frame grab 96 from the students' footage—it's the one from the end of the film, where Heather and Mike are running through the house and run by a wall covered with what looks like hieroglyphics.

Hold it next to the photo from the magazine article on Kyle Brody.

It's the same writing.

It's the same wall.

It's the same house.

The last scene in the kids' footage is in Rustin Parr's house. Which is impossible, because that house burned down in 1941.

Professional Services Center • 2130 Topanga Creek Boulevard • Cummington, VA • 22769-8990
Office: (927) ████ • Local Pager: (927) ████

1

THREE CENTS

THE WASHINGTON PRESS

"All the News That's Fit to Print."

LATE CITY EDITION

VOL.XI — SERVING THE NATION'S CAPITOL — NOVEMBER 22, 1941

HAMBURG HIT ;

Fireside Chat' Two Weeks

organization has been charged with being a Communist Front group.

At the hour all Washington theatres were letting out, police emergency cars and motorcyclists roared through downtown Washington to the White House. The two assaulters were arrested and one picketeer was removed to Emergency Hospital where he was reported slightly injured. The picketing continued.

Tonight's fracas followed one at 2 A. M. when a larger group of soldiers and Marines attacked the pickets, tore up their placards and warned them they would be back if the picketing continued. In an earlier assault the policemen did not interfere. Tonight the assailants were seized and one was charged with simple assault. The police then closed and manned the White House gates for the night.

ROOSEVELT TO TALK TO NATION

'Fireside Chat' Two Weeks From Today Is Substituted for Address Tomorrow

By FRANK L. KLUCKHOHN

Special to The New York Times.

WASHINGTON, May 13—President Roosevelt will make a "fireside chat" to the nation May 27, but will not make his scheduled speech before the Pan American Union Wednesday night, it was announced at the White House today.

This change in plans was interpreted generally to mean that the President has in mind no important announcement on American foreign policy for two weeks and that, at least for this period, he does not contemplate any new type of aid for Britain.

The Executive seldom makes fireside chats except upon important matters, however, and his talk on the 27th is generally expected to present an outline of the current position of the United States as he sees it and the future steps that should be taken.

Mr. Roosevelt completed his seventh day in bed because of illness today, and his widely publicized speech was canceled to give him time to recover 'ully, according to official statements.

Stephen T. Early, White House Secretary, emphasized, however, that the President had never intended his talk before the Pan American Union to be of "world-shaking" importance.

Pressure on President

In informed circles it was understood that the Executive did not intend to be pushed into any important steps and that he considered the present time poor for any an-

WEST GERMANS END 'NIGHTMARE'

The article commented on "the tremendous load of bombs that now can be carried by a single British machine."

In a review of war developments, the newspaper observed that "the hardest blows delivered by the German Air Force in recent weeks have been aimed at British ports and centers of shipbuilding" and also that "the experience of the last war proved that British and United States industry made up for sinkings by U-boats."

21 CIVILIANS KILLED IN RAID ON TURKEY

Envoy Is Expected to Reveal Nazi Plans for Near East—Soviet Move Studied

The article commented on "the tremendous load of bombs that now can be carried by a single British machine."

In a review of war developments, the newspaper observed that "the hardest blows delivered by the German Air Force in recent weeks have been aimed at British ports and centers of shipbuilding" and also that "the experience of the last war proved that British and United States industry made up for sinkings by U-boats."

CHILD KILLER HANGED

By LAWRENCE HATEN

The man behind the "Burkittsville Child Massacre" has been put to death. Rustin Parr, age 38 has been the first man to be hanged in the state of Maryland in eight years.

After a full confession, the small town of Burkittsville, Maryland was pulled into the national spotlight as they held Parr's trial after refusing extradition. Parr pled guilty to the seven murders, showin' little remorse whi' apologizing to the parents of the dead.

Celebration ripped through the town on July 17, the day that Parr was found guilty, though all flags were at half-mast in respect for the dead.

At his sentencing, the ever-quiet Parr reacted little to being sentenced to death. Six days before his sentence would be executed, he gave a press conference in which he told reporters that "voices" made him commit the acts.

President Acts Against Was Present—Place Is Not Disclosed

VICHY PRESS TENSE

Plants of Reich Bases Kept Under Attack in British Bombing

By The Associated Press.

BERLIN, Tuesday, May 13—Reichsfuehrer Hitler has received the French Vice Premier, Admiral François Darlan, in the presence of German Foreign Minister Joachim von Ribbentrop, it was officially announced early today.

The communiqué announcing the meeting did not say where or when it took place.

The announcement said:

"The Fuehrer, in the presence of the Reichsminister of Foreign Affairs, received the vice president of the French Ministerial Council, Admiral Darlan.

Hitler-Stalin Talk Forecast

VICHY, France, May 12 (AP)—Separate meetings of Reichsfuehrer Hitler with Premier Joseph Stalin and Premier Mussolini were considered in diplomatic circles here tonight as likely to result from the current political moves over Europe.

The object of the meetings, these circles said, probably would be complete economic if not military organization of the Axis-dominated Continent.

Observers listed the current shake-up of Spain's civil and military organization and Vice Premier Admiral François Darlan's negotiations with the Germans as indicators of forthcoming conferences of Herr Hitler and Mr. Stalin and Signor Mussolini.

Coal Diggers Stay

Wireless to The New York Times.

VICHY, France, May 12—For the time being it is not possible to separate the two hemispheres in any discussion here of the world situation. That the situation is tense and is likely to remain so, at least until President Roosevelt has spoken, is admitted.

In every newspaper as well as in every conversation the United States and what it may or may not do is a recurrent topic.

There are some here who surmise that it may have been mentioned in Paris during the visit there of Vice Premier Admiral François Darlan, who is expected back in Vichy tomorrow to report to Marshal Henri Philippe Pétain, who himself returned this morning after a few days' rest in his Riviera estate.

A semi-official commentary declared today that the Marshal has expressed his satisfaction to the Admiral with the progress of his negotiations hitherto.

It is understood that another Ad-

AVOIDS WORD 'EMERGENCY'

Arrest of Hess's Aide Forbade Him to Said to Show

By Telephone to Th

BERLIN, May 12—Authoritative quarters in Berlin refused to comment late tonight on a British statement that Rudolf Hess, 47-year-old deputy leader of the National Socialist party and Reichsfuehrer Hitler's personal representative, had bailed out of a Messerschmitt plane near Glasgow, Scotland, and was in the hands of the British authorities. Earlier in the evening the Germans had officially reported Herr Hess to be missing.

The man who, on Sept. 1, 1939, was designated by Herr Hitler as his second choice, next to Reich Marshal Hermann Goering, in the line of succession for leadership of the German State, was last heard of in Augsburg, in Bavaria, on Saturday. He was reported to have taken an airplane there for an unknown destination in violation of Herr Hitler's orders prohibiting him from flying because of physical disability.

THE GERMAN STATEMENT

The news of the mysterious disappearance of Herr Hess was released, forty-eight hours after he had been reported missing, in the following communiqué:

Rudolf Hess has met with an accident.

Party Comrade Hess, who because of a disease that for a y has progressively worsened been categorically forbidden the Fuehrer to continue his ing activities, recently fo means in violation of this c mand to come into possessio an airplane.

WAR DECLARA

TUESD

A laconic announcement f 10 Downing Street gave t astounded world last night news that Rudolf Hess, de leader of the Nazi party in many and the third most po ful figure in the Reich, had ed by parachute in Scotland was in safe custody in a G gow hospital suffering fro broken ankle. The official ment gave no direct explan for the dramatic develop but it was presumed that man who was named at the set of the war by Adolf Hitl his second in succession ha liberately fled Germany.

Herr Hess flew to Scotla a Messerschmitt 110, a pla capable of carrying sufficien for his return to Germany. plane crashed Saturday nig the Duke of Hamilton's estate. flier established his identi the hospital, and the Foreig fice dispatched an attaché t terview him there. [All the going, Page 1, Column 5.]

Berlin issued a commu earlier in the day stating Herr Hess apparently suff

PRESIDENT SEEKS 70-DAY COAL TRUCE, FACT-FINDING BOARD

On Saturday, May 10, about 6 P. M., Party Comrade Hess took off from Augsburg for a flight from which until today he has not yet returned. A letter that he left behind unfortunately indicated, by its incoherence, symptoms of a mental derangement that permits the inference that Comrade Hess became the victim of hallucinations.

The Fuehrer immediately ordered the arrest of the adjutants of Party Comrade Hess, who alone knew of these flights and, knowing of their prohibition by the Fuehrer, did not prevent or immediately report them.

Under the circumstances, the National Socialist movement must regretfully assume that Comrade Hess has crashed or met with an accident somewhere on his flight.

Herr Hess last spoke in public in an official capacity on May 1 as the representative of Herr Hitler at the Labor Day demonstration of the party in Augsburg, where he addressed the congress of the Reich Labor Chamber.

Herr Hess, who also was a member of the German Cabinet as Minister Without Portfolio, was born in Alexandria, Egypt, on April 26, 1894. He became identified with the party in 1921, and in recogni-

CHILD KILLER HANGED

By LAWRENCE HATEN

The man behind the "Burkittsville Child Massacre" has been put to death. Rustin Parr, age 38 has been the first man to be hanged in the state of Maryland in eight years.

After a full confession, the small town of Burkittsville, Maryland was pulled into the national spotlight as they held Parr's trial after refusing extradition. Parr pled guilty to the seven murders, showin' little remorse whi' apologizing to the parents of the dead.

Celebration ripped through the town on July 17, the day that Parr was found guilty, though all flags were at half-mast in respect for the dead.

At his sentencing, the ever-quiet Parr reacted little to being sentenced to death. Six days before his sentence would be executed, he gave a press conference in which he told reporters that "voices" made him commit the acts.

Below, a transcript of a news conference Burkittsville Sheriff Damon Bowers conducted shortly after Parr was found guilty and sentenced to death. Courtesy Burkittsville Historical Society.

BURKITTSVILLE SHERIFF'S OFFICE

November 19, 1941

Sheriff Bowers: All right, fellows--one at a time now. Let's do this in an orderly fashion. Zeke, you first, then Robby, then I'm gonna let the national guys take over.

Do you believe in God, Mr. Parr?

Yes.

Do you think you'll go to heaven, Mr. Parr, and that God will forgive you?

Yes.

Have you spoken with a priest, Mr. Parr?

Yes.

And he's absolved you?

Yes.

Did you ask for forgiveness?

Yes.

Have the parents forgiven you?

Don't know.

Mr. Parr, you've been sentenced to death. Do you feel this is fair?

Yes.

What kind of weapons did you use, Mr. Parr?

Knives.

You're going to be hung in three days, how does it make you feel?

I'm getting paid back for what I did.

Are you afraid, Mr. Parr?

No.

Mr. Parr, why those seven children?

That's what the voices told me.

What kind of voices?

An old woman.

Was it the Blair Witch, Mr. Parr?

Sheriff Bowers: Let's not have any talk like that.

Let the man answer the question. Let him answer the question! Was it the Blair Witch?

I don't know.

Why didn't you kill Kyle Brody? Why'd you let him live?

He wasn't one of them.

What do you mean?

That's what the voices told me.

Were they just voices, Mr. Parr? Did you ever see anyone?

She was a ghost. I never saw her face.

How long have you lived in the woods?

All my life.

How'd you get the children to your house, Mr. Parr?

Promised 'em things.

What kind of things?

Candy.

Have you killed any others?

No.

Mr. Parr, the writing on the walls in your house, what does it mean?

I don't know.

Did you write on those walls?

No.

Who did?

She did. The ghost. The Blair Witch. Whoever you say she was.

What happened to her Mr. Parr? Where did she go?

She's in the woods.

Sheriff Bowers: All right fellows, I think that's enough.

Twenty-five years after the fact, a national news magazine published this retrospective on the Parr Killings.

THE NATION

Addenda To Murder

Our legal system recognizes that there are degrees of evil, even when the crime is murder. Yet even if such shadings were not codified, if all we had to go by was the moral compass of our own hearts, who among us would disagree that the blackest, foulest most unthinkable crime of all is the intentional killing of a child?

Words fail us, then, when we seek to comprehend the depraved mind of the man tried, convicted, and executed for the 1941 murder of seven children in Burkittsville, Maryland. Rustin Parr, born and raised in Burkittsville, was a hermit who lived alone in the woods, miles from any other human, a harmless, twice-a-year visitor to town, a man suddenly compelled -- for reasons which must be forever unknown to us -- to commit one of the foulest crimes of the twentieth century.

RUSTIN PARR'S HOUSE
Burned to the ground by the townspeople of Burkittsville after Parr was hung.

Kyle Brody was the sole survivor of Rustin Parr's murderous rampage. The details are almost too horrible to repeat: nine years old when he was kidnapped, Kyle was forced to stand by, helpless, while Parr killed seven other small children. Eventually, Parr released Brody, whose testimony at Parr's trial helped send the hermit to his death.

But there was to be no happy ending for Kyle Brody. Plagued by recurring nightmares, Brody eventually had to be institutionalized. Today he is a resident of the Reston Hills Sanitarium, in Atlanta, Georgia. Janine Brody, just two years old when her brother was kidnapped, talked with us about the impact Kyle's ordeal had on her family.

Do you remember anything at all about 1941 -- about Rustin Parr?

Not really -- the first memories I have are of a couple years after that, of my mother and father arguing about Kyle, about how to "fix him," my father kept saying. They didn't realize there was no fixing him.

That must have been hard.

It was. Sometimes Kyle was okay. He was my big brother -- just like every other little girl's big brother. He'd watch out for me at school. And then there were times when he wouldn't come out of his room. Not to eat dinner, not to see his friends. I remember one morning I went up to get him to go to school, and he was hiding under his bed. He'd slept there the whole night.

Did he know there was something wrong with him?

That was the hardest part. Kyle did all these things that were crazy, and yet he used to insist there was nothing wrong with him. I'll give you an example -- one Halloween, in

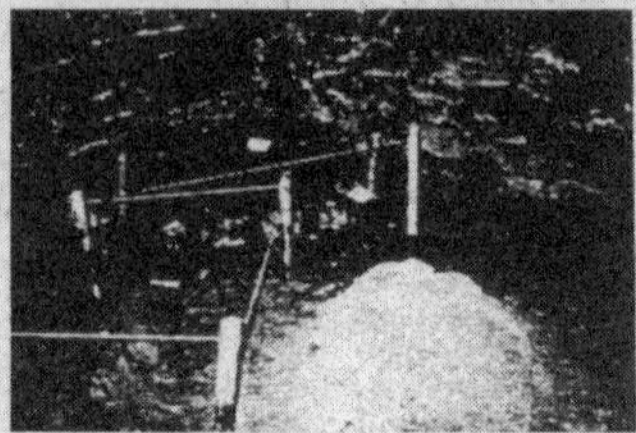

POLICE PHOTOS OF THE CRIME SCENE

between his junior and senior year at high school, I'd invited a whole group of my friends over to the house. He locked all of us in the basement -- wouldn't let us go out at all. He said it was for our own protection -- that Rustin Parr was waiting for us outside. I remember talking with him, reminding him that Parr was dead. And he was shouting at me, practically crying, telling me that it didn't matter, that you couldn't kill Rustin Parr. After that, Kyle got sent away for the first time.

How's Kyle doing now?

He has his good days and his bad ones. You could have a perfectly rational conversation with him one afternoon, and then show up for breakfast with him the next day, and he'll be standing in the room, facing the corner, calling you Rustin, and asking if it's okay to turn around now.

That must be hard for you, not knowing how he's going to be.

Oh, no. Not hard for me. I can go home to my husband. Kyle's who it's hard for.

THE WRITING ON THE HOUSE WALLS
No one was ever able to decipher it -- or the reason for Parr's horrible crimes.

At Parr's trial, he claimed to have committed the murders at the behest of "voices in his head": some locals believed those voices belonged to the Blair Witch, a legend dating back to the late 1700s. This legend begins in 1787, when a woman named Elly Kedward, after being accused of drawing blood from several of the town's children, was banished, literally driven into the wilderness in the dead of winter and abandoned to die. The following summer, those same children began to disappear, victims (supposedly) of Kedward, who came to be known as the Blair Witch. Panick-

One of Parr's victim's shoes, found in his basement.

A political cartoon that ran in the paper the week he was executed.

Hundreds of people gathered to watch Parr being hanged.

BUCHANAN'S
PRIVATE INVESTIGATIVE AGENCY, INC.
Serving Since 1940

This Report Constitutes Confidential Work Product and May Further Constitute Work Product of the Nature of an Attorney-Client Privilege

April 4, 1996
Re: BPIA #94-117

TO: Buck Buchanan

FROM: Carlos Sonenberg

RE: Kyle Brody, Father Dominick Cazale

Brody (the kid who survived Parr's massacre) died in 1971. Cazale is the priest who heard Parr's confession.

The good father is no longer a good father. He gave up the priesthood in 1949, married a young woman from Harrisburg, Pennsylvania, and became a teacher. He also joined the Peace Corps, marched with the Civil Rights movement, was with Chavez in California—you get the idea. They retired to Florida a few years back.

Transcript follows.

Professional Services Center • 2130 Topanga Creek Boulevard • Cummington, VA • 22769-8990
Office: (927) [redacted] • Local Pager: (927) [redacted]

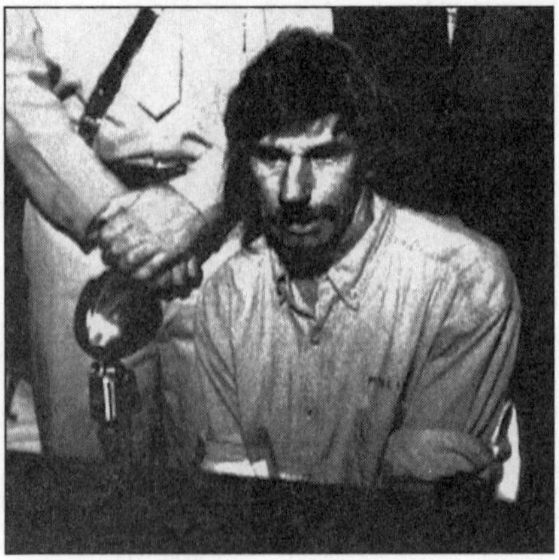

BUCHANAN'S
PRIVATE INVESTIGATIVE AGENCY, INC.
Serving Since 1940

This Report Constitutes Confidential Work Product and May Further Constitute Work Product of the Nature of an Attorney-Client Privilege

March 29, 1996
Re: BPIA #94-117
Transcript of Tape 94-117-124

Carlos Sonenberg: I appreciate you talking to me like this, Mr. Cazale. Do you mind if I tape this conversation for my client?

Dominick Cazale: No. Now what's this client of yours got to do with me?

CS: It's her daughter, sir. She's one of three young people who've gone missing in the Black Hills, near Burkittsville—

DC: Oh dear God. You want to talk about Rustin Parr.

CS: I do.

DC: I tell you, no matter how I try to forget . . .

CS: I'll try to make this brief, Mr. Cazale. You heard his confession?

DC: Yes, of course.

CS: And you absolved him?

DC: Yes, may God have mercy on his poor, unfortunate soul.

CS: You make it sound as if he didn't kill those seven children.

DC: Oh, he did. Rustin did. But he certainly—he believed he didn't do it of his own free will.

CS: What did he tell you?

DC: I won't break the sanctity of the confessional.

CS: But you're not a priest anymore.

DC: No, I'm not. But he spoke to me under the seal of God. That conversation must remain inviolate.

CS: Is there anything he said that—

DC: Young man, I believe I've told you all I'm going to about Rustin Parr.

CS: All right.

DC: Now if you want to ask me about Harrisburg, or the work we did in Mexico—

CS: Tell me about your decision to leave the priesthood.

DC: Hah! You think you're clever?

CS: Sir?

DC: You want to know if Rustin Parr had anything to do with that?

CS: I confess, I do.

DC: Confess—hah! All right—you want to know one thing I took away from my talk with Rustin Parr, young man? I realized how very short life is. I eventually decided to leave the priesthood because I wanted to live my life.

CS: All right.

DC: And don't ask me anything more about that.

CS: No sir, I won't.

DC: Now let me ask you a question—how long have these young people been missing?

CS: Since October 1994.

DC: And there's no possibility they went anyplace else but the Black Hills?

CS: It doesn't look that way, no sir.

DC: [heavy sigh] Well then, I'll pray for them. Is there anything else I can do for you?

CS: I suppose not, sir. If you do change your mind about talking—

DC: I won't.

CS: But if you do, let me give you my number.

DC: No. But you can call me again, if you like. Tell me if you find those kids.

CS: I'll do that, Mr. Cazale. Thank you, sir. Good-bye.

DC: Good-bye.

Professional Services Center • 2130 Topanga Creek Boulevard • Cummington, VA • 22769-8990
Office: (927) ████ • Local Pager: (927) ████

An interview Investigator Sonenberg conducted with Hampshire College Linguistics Professor Peter Walling. It's worth remembering that the letters on Parr's wall that could be discerned from evidence photos and footage makes no sense may simply mean that portions of the original writing were worn away.

BUCHANAN'S

PRIVATE INVESTIGATIVE AGENCY, INC.

Serving Since 1940

This Report Constitutes Confidential Work Product and May Further Constitute Work Product of the Nature of an Attorney-Client Privilege

March 29, 1996
Re: BPIA #94-117
Transcript of Tape 94-117-125

Carlos Sonenberg: Thank you for your help, Professor Walling.

Peter Walling: It's no trouble.

CS: And you don't mind if I tape this conversation?

PW: Not at all.

CS: Good. I'd like to show you a picture with some symbols. I'm hoping you can tell me what they are, and if they mean anything.

PW: I can certainly try.

CS: Let's see . . . this picture here. And this one here, is a close-up of the same thing.

PW: Ah. Well . . . I can tell you what these symbols are—what I think they are.

CS: What are they?

PW: They're so smeared, but . . . yes, they are letters. A Hebraic alphabet. I believe it is Transitus Fluvii.

CS: Hebraic? You mean, Hebrew?

PW: The same basic letters, yes, but . . . that's strange.

CS: What?

PW: Ah, well . . . some of these symbols don't belong. They're not Hebraic at all—they're Futhark.

CS: [laughter] Futhark? What the hell is that?

PW: It's a proto-European language that dates from the first millenium B.C.

CS: That's a funny name for a language.

PW: The name is derived from the letters themselves—like our own alphabet. You know, alpha and beta? The first two letters in the Greek language. The f, u, th, a, r, and k are the first six letters in this language, so—futhark. Inscriptions written in futhark are called runes.

CS: Ah. Now those I've heard of, thanks to Dungeons and Dragons.

PW: [laughter] Exactly. We find runic inscriptions all over in Germany, England, and Ireland, in ruins of the time. Now these symbols in your picture are—well, you see that one in the corner there, next to the hand? That's the symbol for f. The problem is . . . the order. It makes no sense. And some of them . . . hmmm.

CS: What is it?

PW: Well, I'd have to get out my reference books to be sure . . . but now that I look at these symbols closely, some of them aren't exactly right. Or perhaps they're simply drawn differently than usual. Where was this picture taken?

CS: It's part of an ongoing investigation so—I'd rather not say.

PW: Of course. I understand. It's a modern picture though, yes? Someone trying to duplicate the language?

CS: Yes.

PW: And what do the handprints mean?

CS: Again—

PW: Yes, I see. It's part of an investigation.

CS: That's right. Thank you very much for your help, Professor Walling.

PW: I'm not sure that I was any help but . . . you're welcome.

Professional Services Center • 2130 Topanga Creek Boulevard • Cummington, VA • 22769-8990

Office: (927) [redacted] • Local Pager: (927) [redacted]

THE FUTHARK ALPHABET

ᚠ FEHU [f] "material posessions"	ᚢ URUZ [u] "power"	ᚦ THURISAZ [th] "evil, darkness"	ᚨ ANSUZ [a] "divinity"
ᚱ RAIDHO [r] "enlightenment"	ᚲ KENAZ [k,c] "light, spirit"	ᚷ GEBO [g] "sacrifice, gift"	ᚹ WUNJO [w,v] "fortune"
ᚺ HAGALAZ [h] "crystal, snow"	ᚾ NAUHTIZ [n] "destiny"	ᛁ ISA [i] "death"	ᛃ JERA [j,y] "year, season"
ᛇ EIHWAZ [eo] "wood, tree"	ᛈ PERTHRO [p] "rock, earth"	ᛉ ALGIZ [z] "twin"	ᛊ SOWILO [s] "sun, fire"
ᛏ TIWAZ [t] "war"	ᛒ BERKANO [b] "female"	ᛖ EHWAZ [e] "mystery, secret"	ᛗ MANNAZ [m] "male, human"
ᛚ LAGUZ [l] "water, blood"	ᛜ INGWAZ [ng] "birth, fertility"	ᛟ OTHALA [o] "family"	ᛞ DAGAZ [d] "day, air"

Note the final E-mail in the series. Sonenberg refers to the property record included on page 24.

TO: LAURIAT

FROM: BUCK001

DATE: April 8, 1996

I wasn't able to reach you at the Washington number. Let's see if this gets to you before an old-fashioned fax would.

You were right about parallels to the Parr case—but this goes beyond parallels. See the attached files re: Hart's discussion of the killer's methodology and Sonenberg's discovery that the house the students were killed in was a copy of Parr's . . . it seems clear we are dealing with some disturbed individuals here.

I can't help but suspect a very intimate connection to Parr. Can you get me a copy of that Parr family tree you mentioned the Bureau had worked up back in the 40s?

TO: BUCK001

FROM: LAURIAT

DATE: April 9, 1996

Parr family history enclosed herein.

Let me know if there's anything else I can do.

TO: CS
FROM : CDB
DATE: April 9, 1996

Here's a list of Rustin Parr's immediate family. Can you run the names through public record?

KATHLEEN FAGAN
ROBERT TORRINGTON
JAMIE MEYER
VIRGIL MENDON
STANTON PARR
ELAINE HODDY
CONSTANCE SYKES
WILSON PARR
DALE PARR
RUSTIN PARR

Thanks.

TO: CDB
FROM: CS
DATE: April 10, 1996

I spent the last couple of days in the county courthouse digging through old birth certificates, marriage licenses, death certificates, etc. Here's what I found. Parr had a twin brother named Dale, who died in a hunting accident when he was nine years old. His mother—the former Charity Sykes—and his father, Wilson Parr—died within a year of each other in the early thirties. Both Wilson and Charity were only children—Parr had no close blood relatives. With his death, the family line came to an end.

Go back a little further, though, and you find something very interesting.

Charity's parents were Constance Blair (though I suspect one, I can find no connection to the original settlers of the area) and William Sykes. Sykes had a brother named Eldon.

Dig through those property records I copied you on at the beginning of the case. You'll find that in 1858, Eldon Sykes owed the property the students footage was found in. The foundation, the burned-out shell of a house in the woods. . . .

Could those be the remains of Rustin Parr's house?

The truth emerges: Sonenberg's discoveries lead Buck Buchanan to follow up with Sheriff Ron Cravens.

BUCHANAN'S
PRIVATE INVESTIGATIVE AGENCY, INC.
Serving Since 1940

This Report Constitutes Confidential Work Product and May Further Constitute Work Product of the Nature of an Attorney-Client Privilege

May 3, 1996
Re: BPIA #94-117
Transcript of Tape 94-117-144

[CONTINUED]

Ron Cravens: Burkittsville is my town. I was born and raised here, my family lives here, and I am not going to let some smartass New York kid come in and make us look like a bunch of hicks.

C. D. Buchanan: Heather Donahue was not some smart-ass New York kid.

RC: Yeah? Look at how she treated Mary Brown, and Bob Griffin. Made fun of them.

CDB: She was not making fun of them, Sheriff—

RC: I don't care to debate the point with you.

CDB: All right. So you knew it was Parr's house where they found the footage.

RC: That's right.

CDB: And you didn't say anything.

RC: You're damn right I didn't! What good would it have done for the news people to be jumping up and down about that whole mess again? It'd be like the damn horror movies where that kid in the hockey mask keeps coming back to life. Besides, I was on top of every single one of those clues that led to Parr, and to anybody connected to him. They didn't tell me anything.

CDB: So at this point?

RC: I have no leads. None.

CDB: What about the fact that the house is in the footage, and—

RC: All right, so they built a copy of the house for their movie—I don't know. That's the best I can come up with.

CDB: Yeah. That's where I am, too.

[CONTINUED]

Professional Services Center • 2130 Topanga Creek Boulevard • Cummington, VA • 22769-8990
Office: (927) [redacted] • Local Pager: (927) [redacted]

HEATHER'S JOURNAL

Diane Ahlquist. A third-generation psychic, Diane has worked with law-enforcement authorities across the country, and was brought in to work on the case by Buck Buchanan at Angela Donahue's request.

April 16, 1999

Angela Donahue

Dear Angela:

I'm sorry it's taken me so long to get back to you: I have been staying in New Mexico with friends. Luckily, I'm having my mail forwarded, and so I received your letter today.

I am so sorry to hear about your daughter: it sounds as if the last few years have been extremely difficult ones for you and your family. I sense you have a strong and resilient spirit—I know that will continue to serve you well.

I'm flattered that Buck Buchanan remembered me, and thought I might be of some assistance in your case. My trip here is expected to last until the second week of May, but if you're willing, I think I can get started in trying to help you sooner. I will be at 505- this weekend: if you could call me then, we can talk in more detail about "exactly what I do," as you put it.

Sincerely,

Diane Ahlquist

Dear Diane,

It was good to talk to you last night, and I am so glad you are willing to work on this case.

You asked for something of my daughter's that was particularly important to her.

I'm sending you the journal she kept while she was filming her movie. If anything bears a trace of her energy - for lack of a better word - it would be this. You'll see - particularly in her last few days - that even while she was writing it, she seemed to think it might survive her, that it might serve as some kind of clue as to what happened to her, Michael, and Josh. I hope it will.

I'm going to sound like an old mother when saying this, but I have to: forgive me. Please take good care of this: it's the last thing of hers I have.

Sincerely,

Angela Donahue

Below and following pages: Heather Donahue's journal. Diane went through the journal several times, attaching her comments with Post-it notes throughout. I've included the ones Angela held on to, as well as a transcription of the journal itself.

COVER

SATURN—onyx, lead, [mole]

Places ruled: vaults, tombs, monasteries, empty houses, caves, dens, pits

angel—Zapkiel, intelligence—Agiel Spirit—[Sabathiel]

FRANKENSENSE/PEPPERWORT, LEAVES—BAY LEAVES/MYRTLE

moon—cat, silver, pearls wilderness, woods, rocks, forests, ships, highways.

Angel—Gabriel

Intelligence—[Elirriel]

Spirit—Lemanael

moon—monday saturn—saturday moon and saturn very similar, both very nocturna; leader, silver

PAGE 1

Hey, that's a mean looking witch! Yee haw! Let's shoot 'er!

BLAIR WITCH SHOOTING

LOCATION WEEKEND

OCTOBER 1994

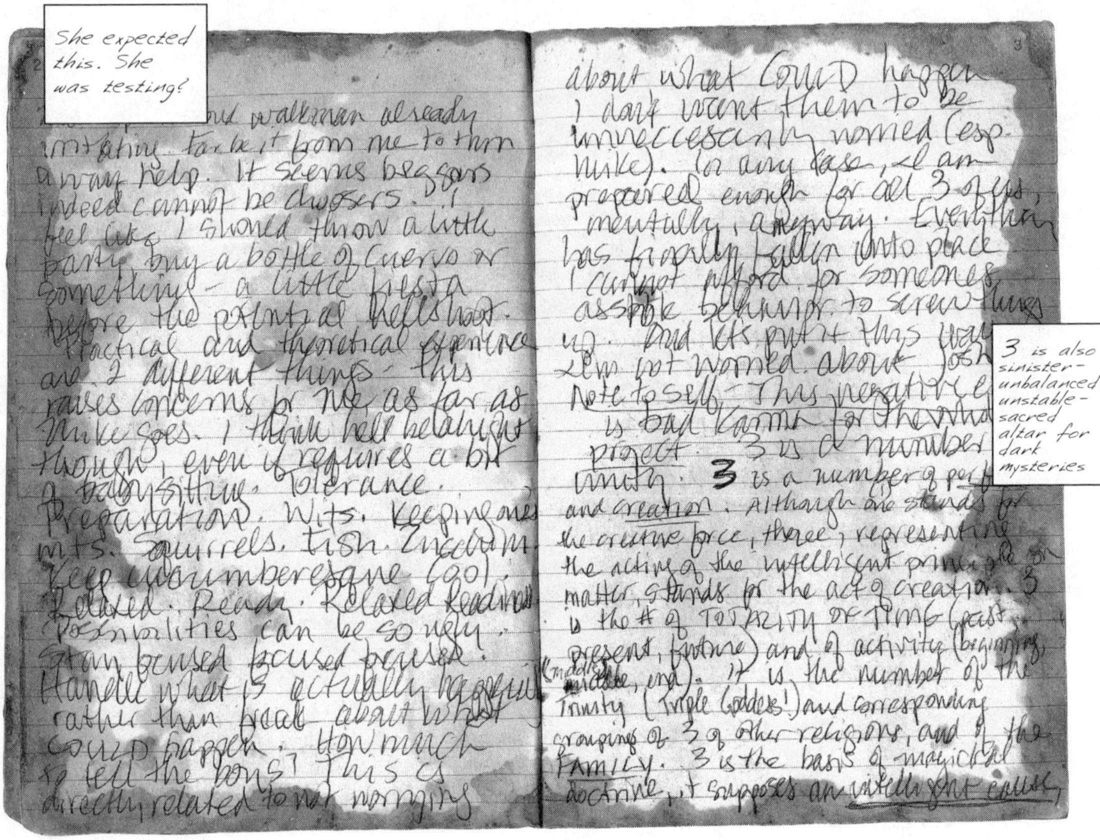

PAGE 2
10/16/94

[?] trip. Too loud walkman already irritating me. Far be it from me to turn away help. It seems beggars can't be choosers. I feel like I should throw a little party, buy a bottle of cuervo or something—a little fiesta before the potential hellshoot. Practical and theoretical experience are 2 different things. This raises concerns for me, as far as Mike goes. I don't know him, but I think he'll be alright though. Tolerance. Preparation. Wits. Keeping one's wits. Squirrels. Fish. [Inuhim]. Keep [ucumberesque] Cool. Relaxed. Ready. Relaxed Readiness. Possibilities can be so ugly. Stay focused focused focused. Handle what is actually happening rather than freak about what would happen. How much to tell the boys? This is directly related to not worrying . . .

PAGE 3

. . . about what could happen. I don't want them to be unnecessarily worried (esp. Mike). For any cases, I am prepared enough for all three of us, mentally, anyway. Everything has finally fallen into place. I cannot afford for someones asshole behavior to screw things up. And let's put it this way, I'm not worried about Josh.

Note to self—This negative energy is bad Karma for the whole project. 3 is a number of unity. 3 is a number of *perfection* and *creation*. Although one (1) stands for the creative force, three, representing the acting of the intelligent principle on matter, stands for the act of creation. 3 is the # of TOTALITY OF TIME (past, present, future) and of activity (beginning, middle, end). It is the number of the Trinity (Triple Goddess!) and corresponding groupings of 3 of other religions, and of the FAMILY. 3 is the basis of magical doctrine, it supposes an intelligent *cause*. . . .

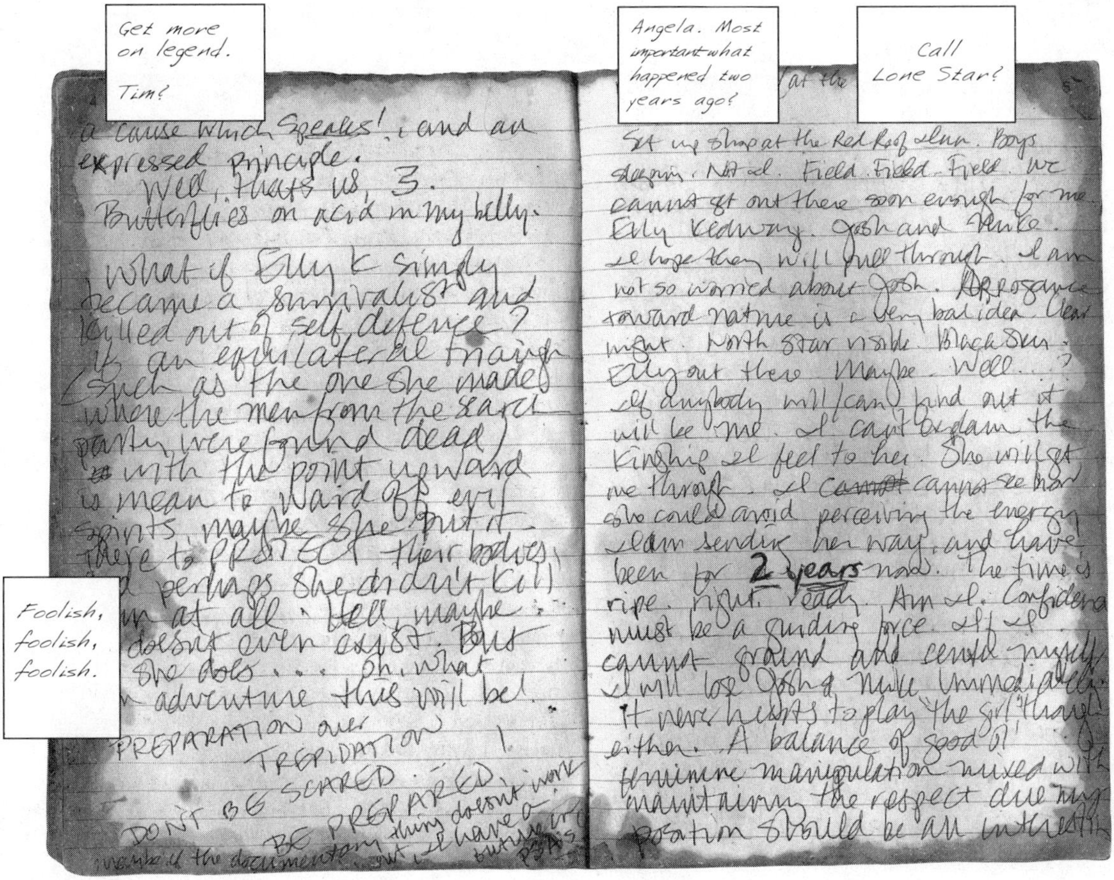

PAGE 4
10/16/94

. . . a cause which speaks!, and an expressed principle. Well, that's us, 3. Butterflies on acid in my belly. What if Elly K simply became a survivalist and killed out of self defense? if an equilateral triangle (such as the one she made where the men from the search party were found dead) with the point upward is mean to ward off evil spirits, maybe she put it there to PROTECT their bodies, and perhaps she didn't kill them at all. Hell, maybe she doesn't even exist. But if she does . . . oh, what an adventure this will be!

PREPARATION over TREPIDATION DON'T BE SCARED . . . BE PREPARED! maybe if the documentary thing doesn't work out, I have a future in PSA's1

PAGE 5
10/16/94 (after the Lone Star)

Set up shop after the Lone Star. Bill sleeping. Not I. Field. Field. Field. We cannot go out there soon enough for me. Elly Kedward. Josh and Mike. I hope they will pull through. I am not so worried about Josh. Arrogance toward nature is a very bad idea. Clear night. North star visible. Black sky. Elly out there. Maybe. Well . . . ? If anything will/can find out it will be me. I can't explain the kinship I feel to her.

She will get through. I cannot see how she could avoid perceiving the energy I am sending her way, and have been for 2 years now. The time is ripe. right. Am I. Confidence must be a guiding force. If I cannot ground and center myself I will lose Josh & Mike immediately. It never hurts to play "the girl" though, either. A balance of good ol' feminine manipulation mixed with maintaining the respect due my position should be an interesting . . .

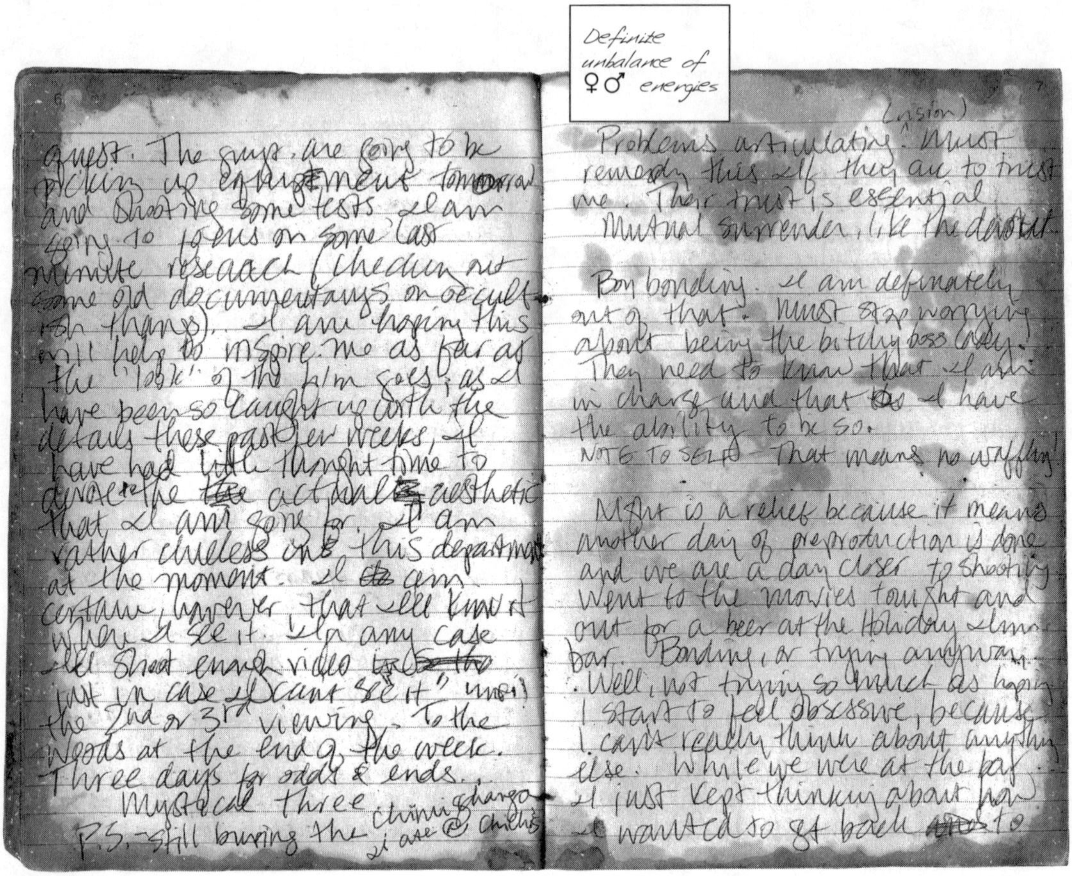

PAGE 6

. . . quest. The guys are going to be picking up equipment tomorrow and shooting some tests. I am going to focus on some last minute research (checking out some old documentarys on occultish things). I am hoping this will help to inspire me as far as the "look" of the film goes, as I have been so caught up with the details these past few weeks. I have had little thought to devote to the actual aesthetic that I am going for. I am rather clueless in this department at the moment. I am certain, however, that I'll know it when I see it. In any case I'll shoot enough video just in case I can't see "it" until the 2nd or 3rd viewing. To the woods at the end of the week. Three days of odds & ends.

Mystical three . . .

P.S.—Still burping the chimi changa I ate at ChiChi's.

PAGE 7
10/17

Problems articulating (vision). Must remedy this if they are to trust me. Their trust is essential. Mutual surrender, like the devout.

Boy bonding. I am definately out of that. Must stop worrying about being the bitchy boss lady. They need to know that I am in charge and that I have the ability to be so.

NOTE TO SELF—That means no waffling!

Night is a relief because it means another day of preproduction is done and we are a day closer to shooting. Went to the movies tonight and out for a beer at the Holiday Inn. Bonding, or trying to anyway. Well, not trying so much as hoping I start to feel obsessive, because I can't really think about anything else. While we were at the bar I just kept thinking about how I wanted to get back to . . .

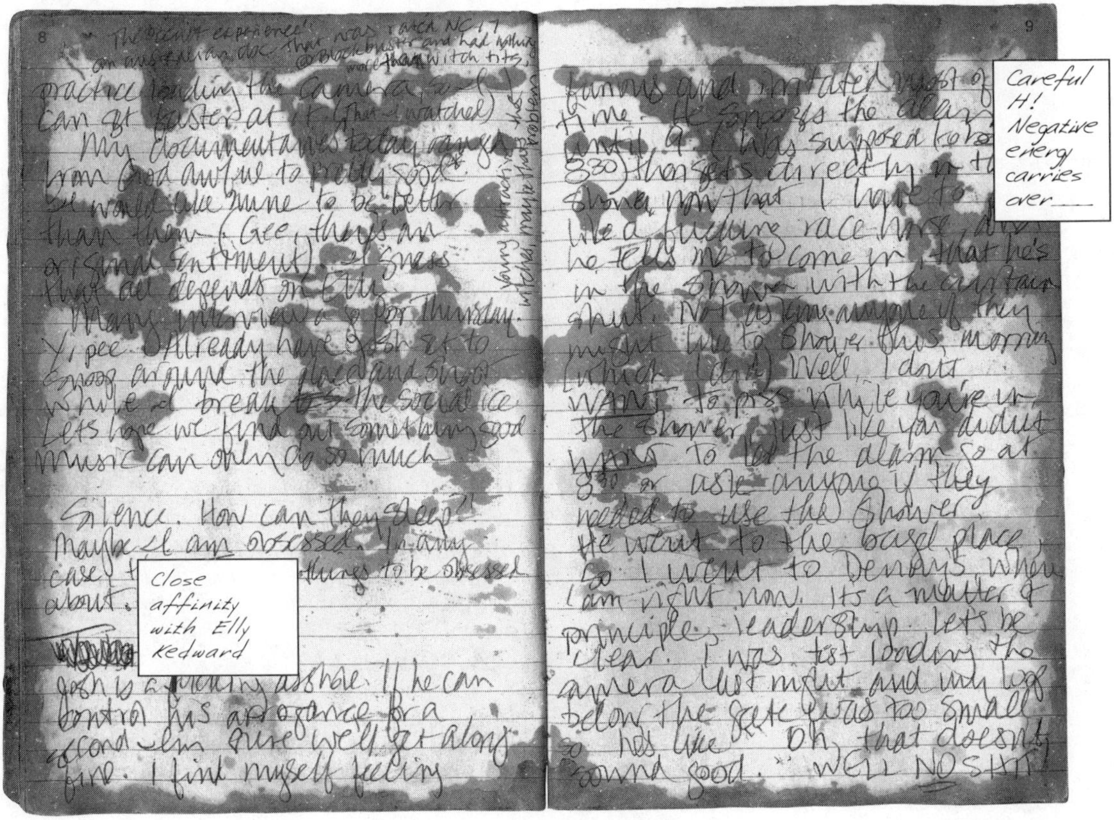

PAGE 8

(Top of page) "The occult experience" an australian doc that was rated NC17 @ Blockbuster and had nothing more than witch tits. Young attractive witches, maybe that's the problem.

. . . practice loading the camera, so I can get faster at it.

My documentaries (That I watched) today ranged from God awful to good. I would like mine to be better than them (Gee, there's an original sentiment). I guess that all depends on Elly.

Mary interview a go for Thursday. Yipee. Already have Josh set to snoop around the place and shoot while I break the social ice. Let's hope we find out something good. Music can only do so much.

Silence. How can they sleep?! Maybe I am obsessed. In any case there are worse things to be obsessed about.

October 18

John [her new roommate at the time] is a fucking asshole. If he can control his arrogance for a second I'm sure we'll get along fine. I find myself feeling . . .

PAGE 9

. . . furious and irritated most of the time. He snoozes the alarm until 9 (was supposed to be 8:30) then gets directly in the shower now that I have to piss like a fucking racehorse, and he tells me to come in, that he's in the shower with the curtain shut. Not asking anyone if they might like to shower this morning (which I did). Well, I don't WANT to piss while you're in the shower, just like you didn't WANT to let the alarm go at 8:30 or ask anyone if they needed to use the shower. He went to the bagel place, so I went to Denny's, where I am right now. It's a matter of principle, leadership. Let's be clear. I was test loading the camera last night and my loop below the gate was too small so he's like "Oh, that doesn't sound good." WELL NO SHIT!

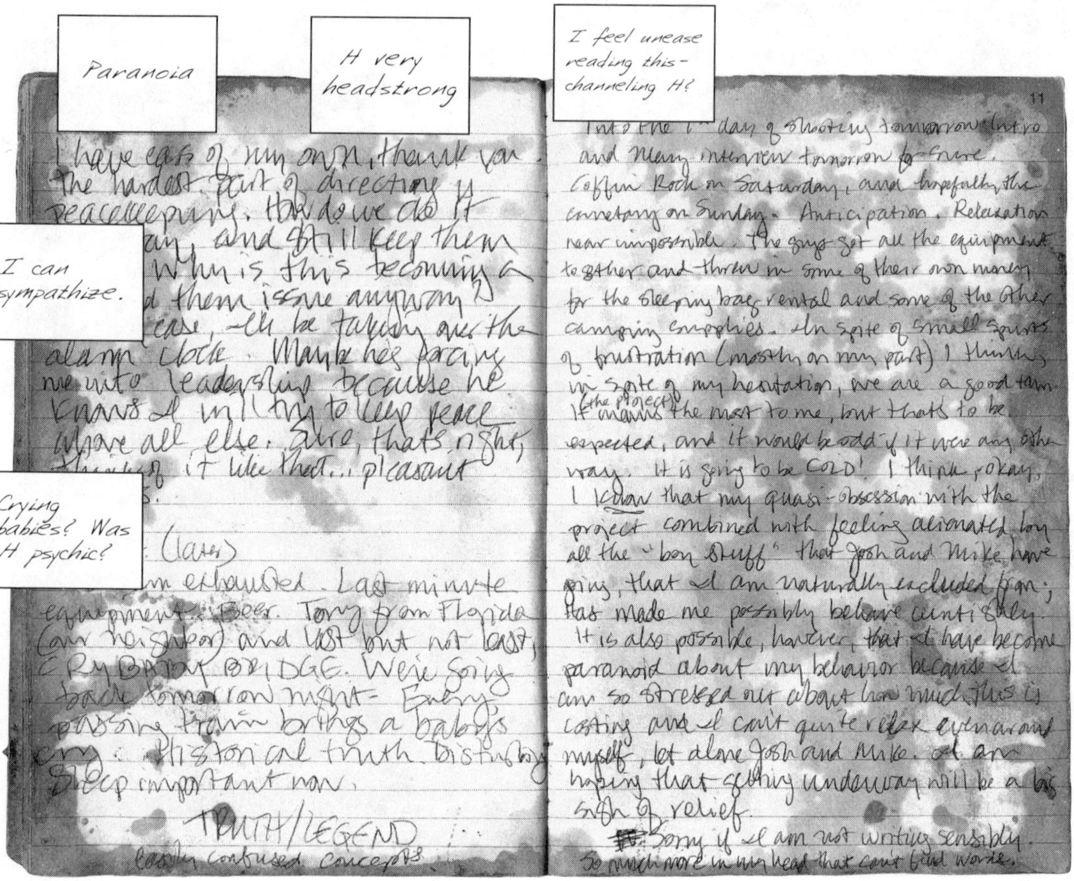

PAGE 10
10/18/94

I have ears of my own, thank you. The hardest part of living together is peacekeeping. How do we do it my way, and still keep him on? Why is it becoming a me and him issue anyway? In any case, I'll be taking over the alarm clock. Maybe he's forcing me into leadership because he know I will try to keep peace above all else. Sure, that's right, think of it like that . . . pleasant thoughts.

10/18/94 (later)

I am exhausted. Last minute equipment. Beer. Tony from Florida (our neighbor) and last but not least, CRY BABY BRIDGE. We're back tomorrow night—Every passing train brings a baby's cry. Historical truth. Disturbing. Sleep important right now.

TRUTH/LEGEND
easily confused concepts

PAGE 11
10/19

Into the 1st day of shooting tomorrow. Intro and Mary interview tomorrow for sure.

Coffin Rock on Saturday, and hopefully the cemetary on Sunday. Anticipation. Relaxation near impossible. The guys got all the equipment together and threw in some of their own money for sleeping bag rental and some of the other camping supplies. In spite of small spurts of frustration (mostly on my part) I think, in spite of my hesitation, we are a good team. It (the project) means the most to me, but that's to be expected, and it would be odd if it were any other way. It is going to be cold! I think, okay, I know that my quasi-obsession with the project combined with feeling alienated by all the "boy stuff" that Josh and Mike will have going, that I am naturally excluded from, will make me possibly behave cuntishly. It is also possible, however, that I have become paranoid about my behavior because I am so stressed out about how much this is costing and I can't quite relax even around myself, let alone Josh and Mike. I am hoping that getting underway will be a big sigh of relief.

Sorry if I am not writing sensibly. So much more in my head that can't find words.

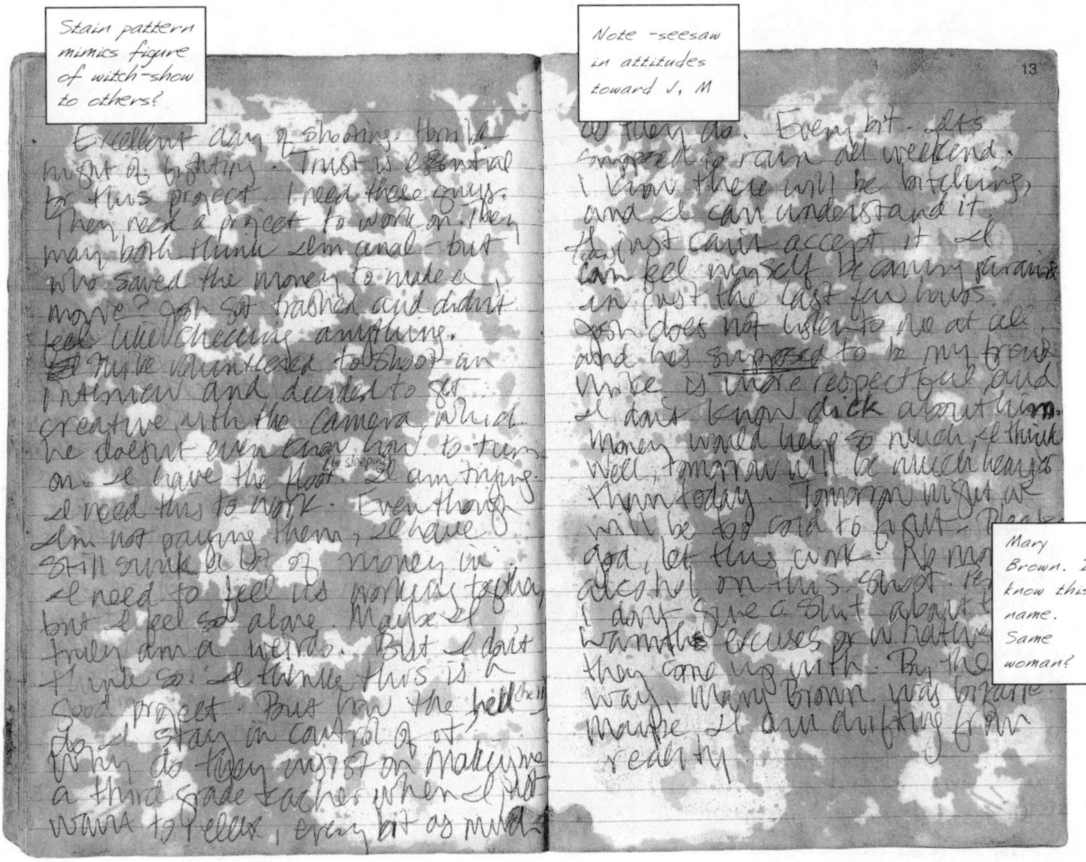

PAGE 12
10/20

Excellent day of shooting. Horrible night of fighting. Trust is essential for this project. I need these guys. They need a project to work on. They may both think I'm anal—but who saved the money to make a movie? Josh got trashed and didn't feel like checking anything. Mike volunteered to shoot an interview and decided to get creative with the camera, which he doesn't even know how to turn on.

I have the floor (for sleeping). I am trying. I need this to work. Even though I'm not paying them, I have still sunk a lot of money in. I need to feel us working together, but I feel so alone. Maybe I truly am a weirdo. But I don't think so. I think this is a good project. But how the hell (hell) do I stay in control of it? Why do they insist on making me a third grade teacher when I just want to relax every bit as much . . .

PAGE 13
10/20

. . . as they do. Every bit. It's supposed to rain all weekend. I know there will be bitching, and I can understand it. I just can't accept it. I can feel myself becoming paranoid in just the last few hours. Josh does not listen to me at all and he's supposed to be my friend. Mike is more respectful and I don't know dick about him. Money would help so much, I think.

Well tomorrow will be much harder than today. Tomorrow night we will be too cold to fight. Please God, let this work. No more alcohol on this shoot. Period.

I don't give a shit about their warmth excuses or whatever else they come up with. By the way, Mary Brown was bizarre. Maybe I am drifting from reality.

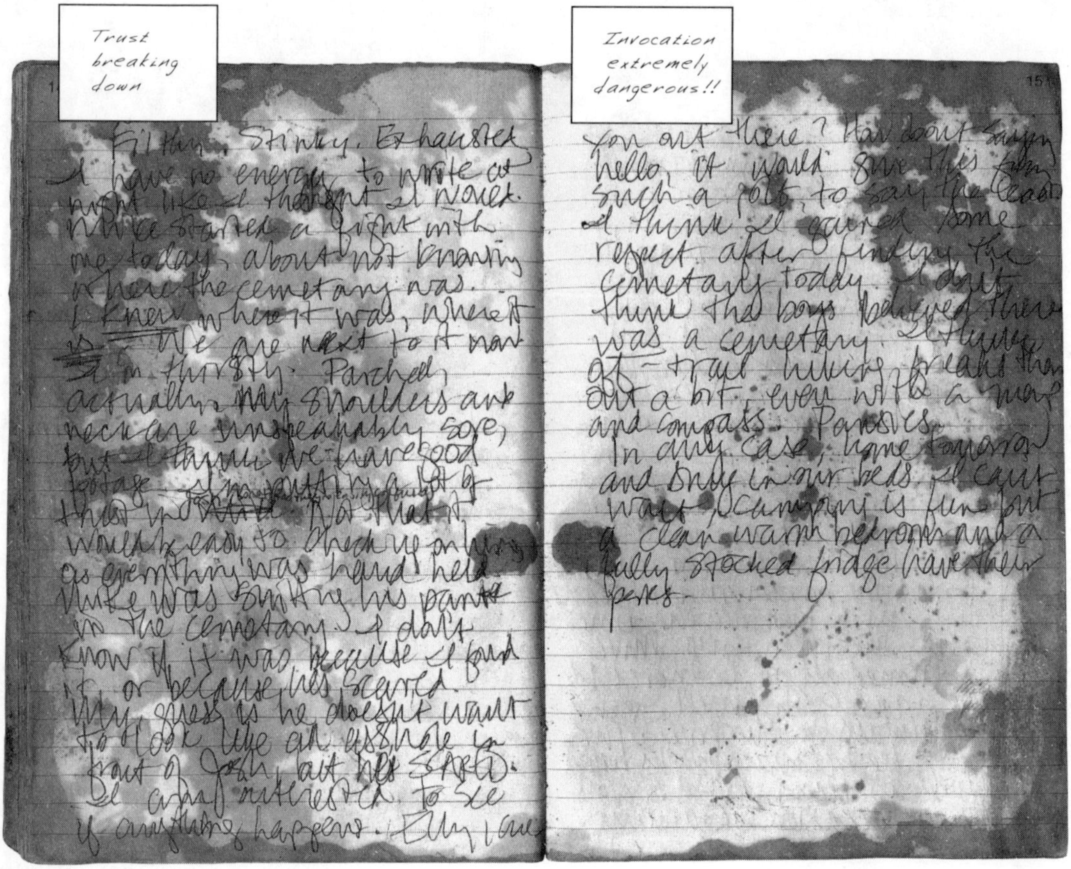

PAGE 14
10/22

Filthy. Stinky. Exhausted. I have no energy to write at night like I thought I would. Mike started a fight with me today, about not knowing where the cemetary was. I knew where it was, where it is. We are next to it now. I'm thirsty. Parched, actually. My shoulders and neck are unspeakably sore, but I think we have good footage. I'm putting a lot of trust in Mike Josh (sometimes they're so easily confused). Not that it would be easy to check up on him as everything was hand held. Mike was shitting his pants in the cemetary. I don't know if it was because I found it or because he's scared. My guess is he doesn't want to look like an asshole in front of Josh, but he's SCARED. I am interested to see if anything happens. Elly, are . . .

PAGE 15
10/22

. . . you out there? How about saying hello, it would give this film such a jolt, to say the least. I think I gained some respect after finding the cemetary today. I don't think the boys believed there was a cemetary. I think off-trail hiking freaked them out a bit even with a map and compass. Pansies.

In any case, home tomorrow and snug in our beds. I can't wait, camping is fun but a clean warm bedroom and a fully stocked fridge have their perks.

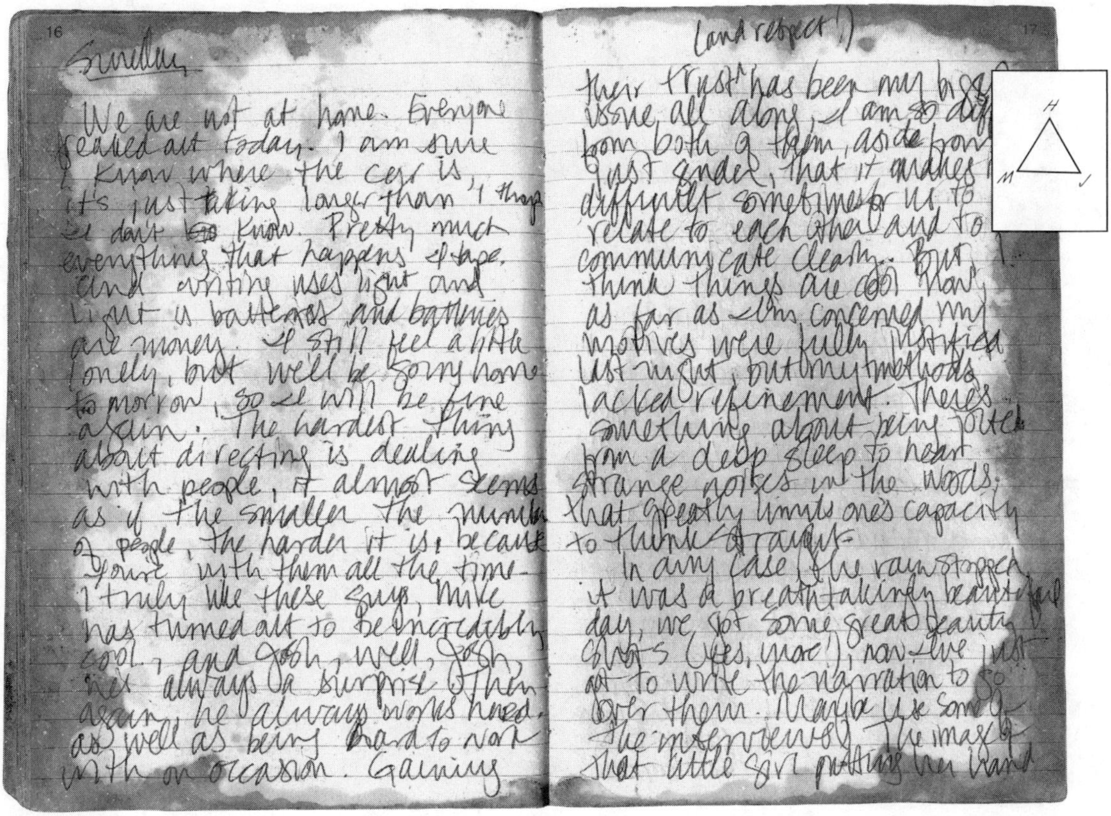

PAGE 16

Sunday

We are not at home. Everyone freaked out today. I am sure I know were the car is, it's just taking longer than I thought. I don't know. Pretty much everything that happens I tape, and writing uses light and light is batteries and batteries are money. I still feel a little lonely, but we'll be going home tomorrow, so I will be fine again. The hardest thing about directing is dealing with people, it almost seems as if the smaller the number of people, the harder it is, because you're with them all the time. I truly like these guys, Mike has turned out to be incredibly cool, and Josh, well, Josh, he's always a surprise. Then again, he always works hard, as well as being hard to work with on occasion. Gaining . . .

PAGE 17

. . . their trust (and respect) has been my biggest issue all along. I am so different from both of them, aside from just gender, that it makes it difficult sometimes for us to relate to each other and to communicate clearly. But, I think things are cool now, as far as I'm concerned my motives were fully justified last night. but my methods lacked refinements. There's something about being jolted from a deep sleep to hear strange noises in the woods, that greatly limits one's capacity to think straight.

In any case, the rain stopped, it was a breathtakingly beautiful night. We got some great beauty shots today (yes, more!), now I've just got to write the narration to go with them. Maybe use some of the interviews. The image of that little girl putting her hand . . .

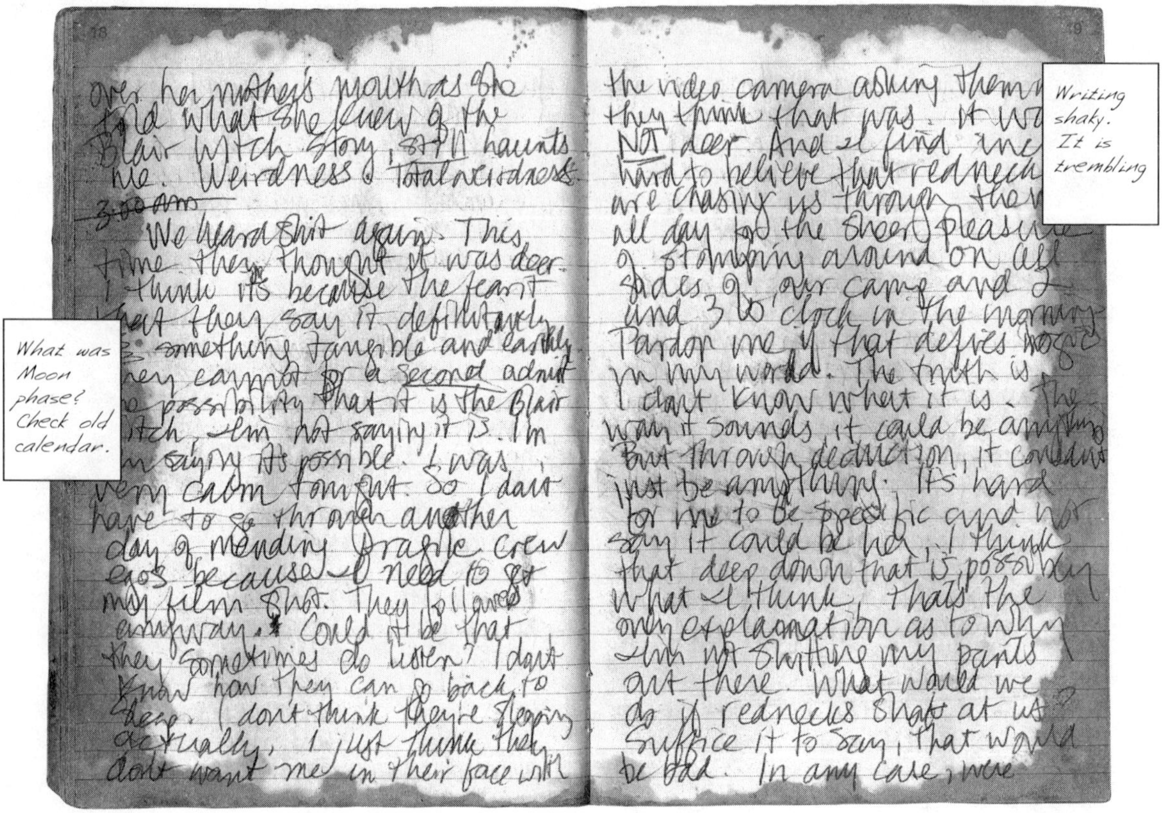

PAGE 18

. . . over her mother's mouth as she told what she knew of the Blair Witch story still haunts me. Weirdness. Total weirdness.

3:00am

We heard shit again. This time they thought it was deer. I think it's because they fear it that they say it definitively is something tangible and earthly. They cannot for a second admit the possibility that it is the Blair Witch. I'm not saying it is. I'm only saying it's possible. I was very calm tonight. So I don't have to go through another day of mending fragile crew egos because I need to get my film shot. They followed anyway. Could it be that they sometimes do listen? I don't know how they can go back to sleep. I don't think they're sleeping actually. I just think they don't want me in their face with . . .

PAGE 19

. . . the video camera asking them what they think that was. It was NOT deer. And I find it incredibly hard to believe that rednecks are chasing us through the woods all day for the sheer pleasure of stomping around on all sides of our camp at 2 and 3 o'clock in the morning.

Pardon me if that defies logic in my world. The truth is I don't know what it is. The way is sounds it could be anything. But through deduction, it couldn't just be anything. It's hard for me to be specific and not say it could be her, I think that deep down that is possibly what I think, that's the only explanation as to why I'm not shitting my pants out there. What would we do if rednecks shot at us? Suffice it to say, that would be bad. In any case, we're . . .

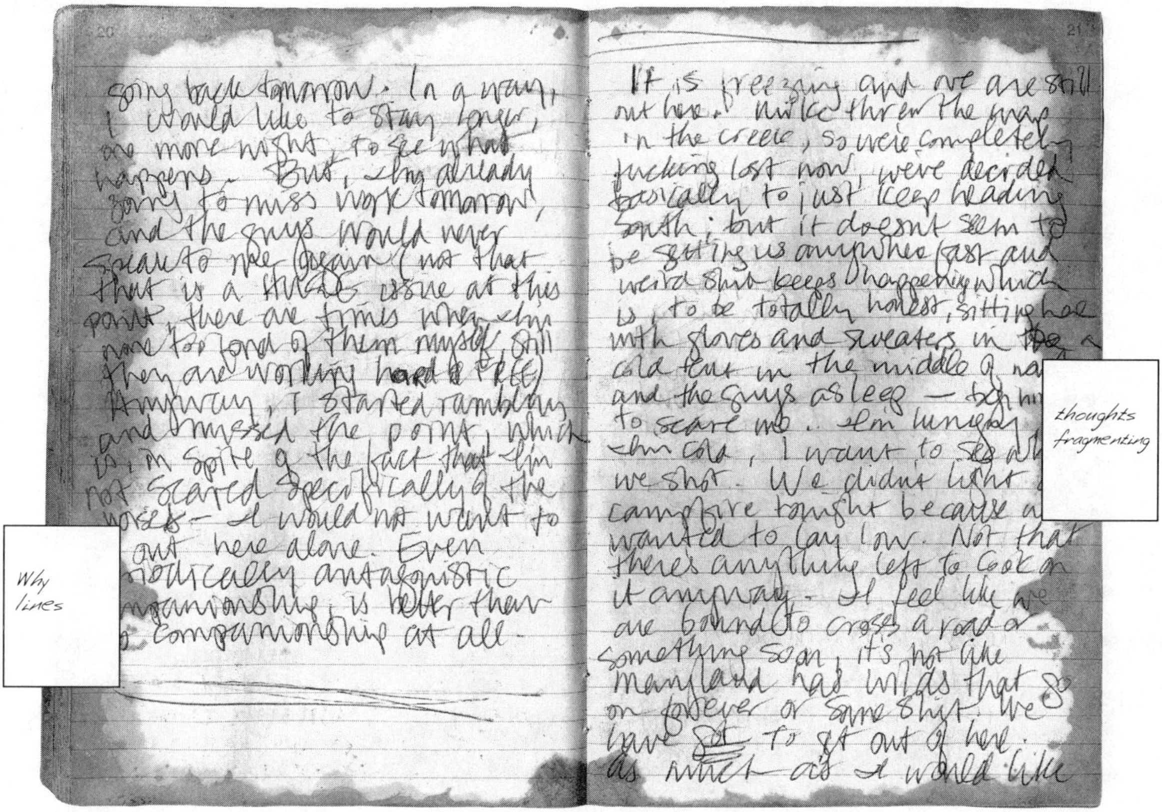

PAGE 20

. . . going back tomorrow. In a way, I would like to stay longer, one more night, to see what happens. But, I'm already going to miss work tomorrow, and the guys would never speak to me again (not that that is a HUGE issue at this point, there are times when I'm not too fond of them myself. Still they are working hard & FREE) Anyway, I started rambling and missed the point, which is, in spite of the fact that I'm not scared specifically of the noises—I would not want to be out here alone. Even periodically antagonistic companionship is better than no companionship at all.

PAGE 21

It is freezing and we are still out here. We're completely fucking lost now, we've decided basically to just keep heading south, but it doesn't seem to be getting us anywhere fast and weird shit keeps happening which is, to be totally honest, sitting here with gloves and sweaters in a cold tent in the middle of nowhere and the guys asleep—beginning to scare me. I'm hungry. I'm cold. I want to see what we shot. We didn't light a campfire tonight because we wanted to lay low. Not that there's anything left to cook on it anyway. I feel like we are bound to cross a road or something soon, it's not like Maryland has wilds that go on forever or some shit. We have got to get out of here. As much as I like . . .

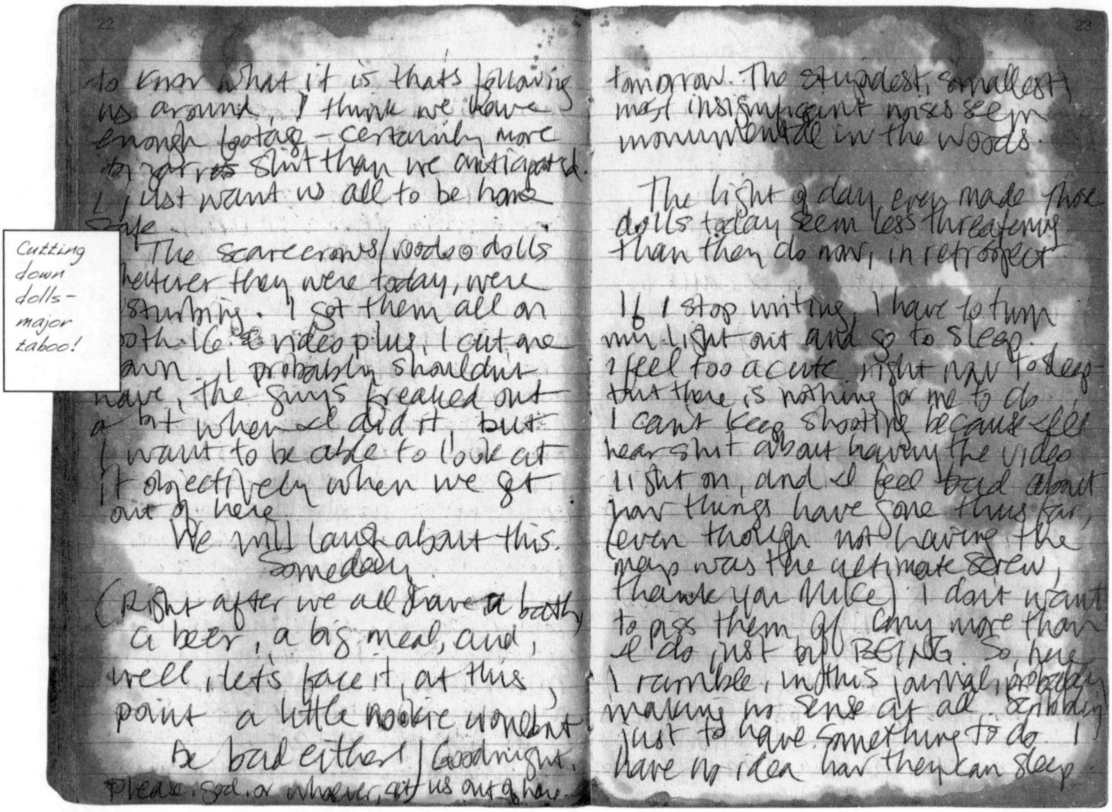

PAGE 22

. . . to know what it is that's following us around. I think we have enough footage—certainly more bizarre shit than we anticipated. I just want us all to be home safe.

The scarecrows/voodoo dolls whatever they were today, were disturbing. I got them all on both 16 & video plus, I cut one down. I probably shouldn't have, the guys freaked out a bit when I did it, but I want to be able to look at it objectively when we get out of here.

We will laugh about this someday.

(Right after we all have a bath, a beer, a big meal, and, well, let's face it, at this point a little nookie wouldn't be bad either) Good night. Please, God, or whatever, get us out of here . . .

PAGE 23

. . . tomorrow. The stupidest, smallest, most insignificant noises seem monumental in the woods.

The light of day even made those dolls today seem less threatening than they do now, in retrospect.

If I stop writing, I have to turn my light out and go to sleep. I feel too acute right now to sleep, but there is nothing for me to do. I can't keep shooting because I'll hear shit about having the video light on, and I feel bad about how things have gone thus far (even though not having the map was the ultimate screw). I don't want to piss them off any more than I do just by BEING. So here I ramble in this journal, probably making no sense at all. Scribbling just to have something to do. I have no idea how they can sleep.

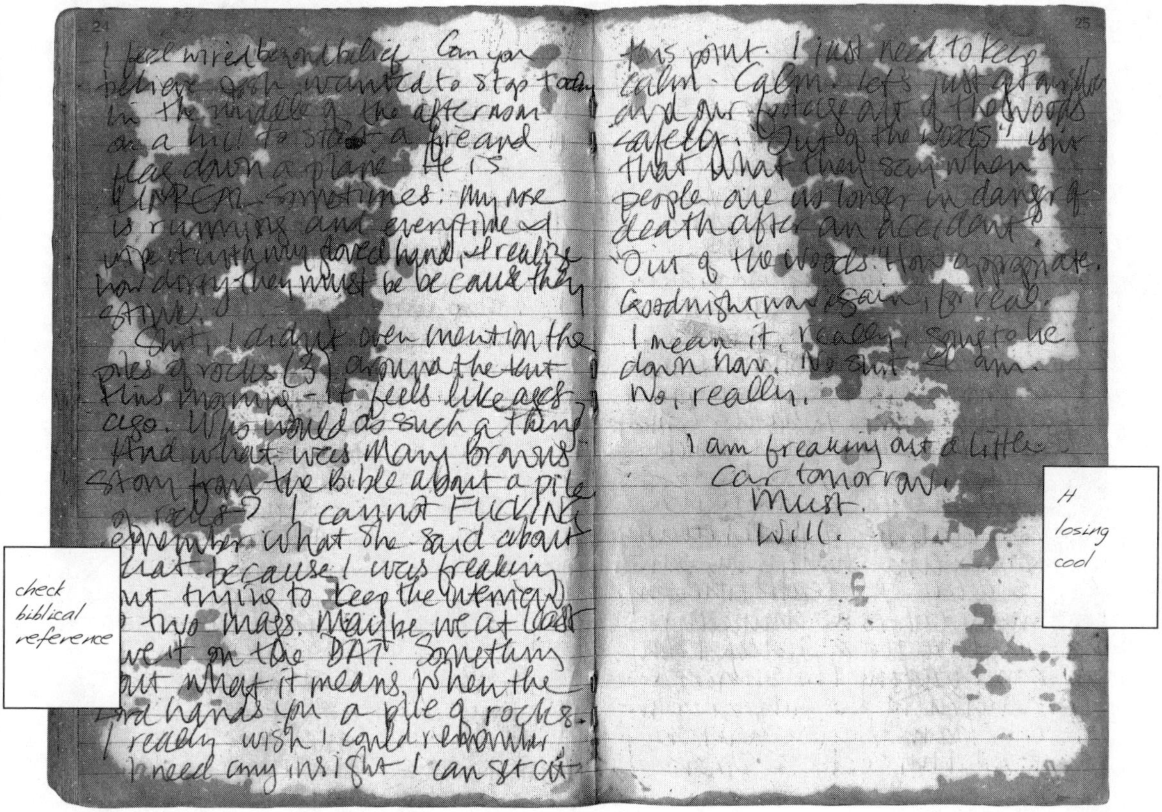

PAGE 24

. . . I feel wired beyond belief. Can you believe Josh wanted to stop today in the middle of the afternoon on a hill to start a fire and flag down a plane. He is UNREAL sometimes. My nose is running and everytime I wipe it with my gloved hand, I realize how dirty they must be because they stink.

Shit, I didn't even mention the piles of rocks (3) around the tent this morning—it feels like ages ago. Who would do such a thing? And what was Mary Brown's story from the Bible about a pile of rocks? I cannot FUCKING remember what she said about that because I was freaking out trying to keep the interview to two mags. Maybe we at least have it on the DAT. Something about what it means when the Lord hands you a pile of rocks. I really wish I could remember. I need any insight I can get at . . .

PAGE 25

. . . this point. I just need to keep calm. Calm. Let's just get ourselves and our footage out of the woods safely. "Out of the woods" isn't that what they say when people are no longer in danger of death after an accident? "Out of the woods." How appropriate. Goodnight, now again, for real. I mean it, really, going to lie down now. No shit. I am. No, really.

I am freaking out a little.

Car tomorrow.

Must.

Will.

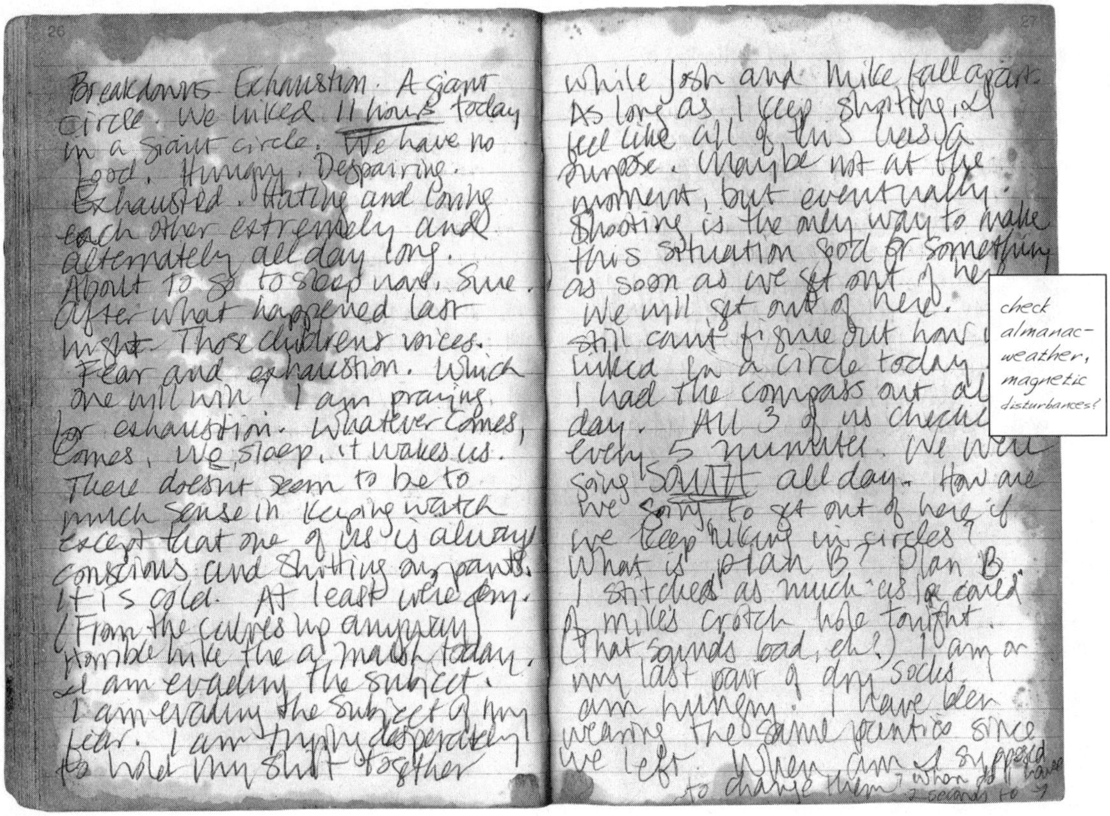

PAGE 26

Breakdowns. Exhaustion. A giant circle. We hiked 11 hours today in a giant circle. We have no food. Hungry. Despairing. Exhausted. Hating and loving each other extremely and alternately all day long. About to go to sleep now. Sure. After what happened last night. Those children's voices. Fear and exhaustion. Which one will win? I am praying for exhaustion. Whatever comes, comes. We sleep, it wakes us. There doesn't seem to be to much sense in keeping watch except that one of us is always conscious and shitting our pants. It is cold. At least we're dry (From the calves up anyway). Horrible hike through a marsh today. I am evading the subject. I am evading the subject of my fear. I am trying desperately to hold my shit together . . .

PAGE 27

. . . while Josh and Mke fall apart. As long as I keep shooting, I feel like all of this has a purpose. Maybe not at the moment but eventually. Shooting is the only way to make this situation good for something as soon as we get out of here. We will get out of here. I still can't figure out how we hiked in a circle today. I had the compass out all day. All 3 of us checked it every 5 minutes. We were going SOUTH all day. How are we going to get out of here if we keep hiking in circles? What is plan B? Plan B. I stitched as much as I could of Mike's crotch hole tonight (That sounds bad, eh?). I am on my last pair of dry socks. I am hungry. I have been wearing the same panties since we left. When am I supposed to change them? When do I have 2 seconds to . . .

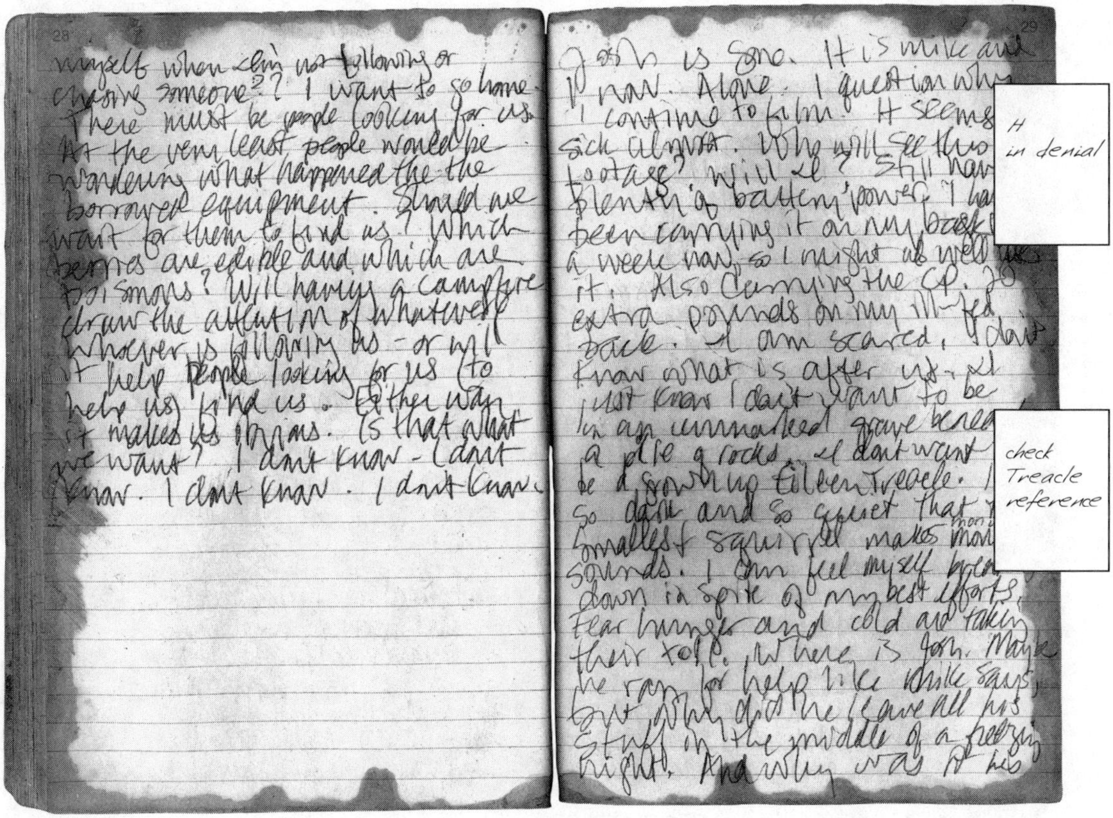

PAGE 28

. . . myself when I'm not following or chasing someone? I want to go home, there must be people looking for us. At the very least people would be wondering what happened to the borrowed equipment. Should we wait for them to find us? Which berries are edible and which are poisonous? Will having a campfire draw the attention of whatever, whoever is following us—or will it help people looking for us (to help us) find us. Either way it makes us obvious. Is that what we want? I don't know—I don't know. I don't know. I don't know.

PAGE 29

Josh is gone. It is Mike and I now. Alone. I question why I continue to film. It seems sick almost. Who will see this footage? Will I? Still have plenty of battery power. I have been carrying it on my back for a week now, so I might as well use it. Also carrying the CP. 20 extra pounds on my ill-fed back.

I am scared. I don't know what is after us. I just know I don't want to be in an unmarked grave beneath a pile of rocks. I don't want to be a grownup Eileen Treacle. It is so dark and so quiet that the smallest squirrel makes monumental sounds. I can feel myself breaking down in spite of my best efforts. Fear, hunger and cold are taking their toll. Where is Josh? Maybe he ran off for help like Mike says, but why did he leave all his stuff in the middle of the freezing night. And why was it his . . .

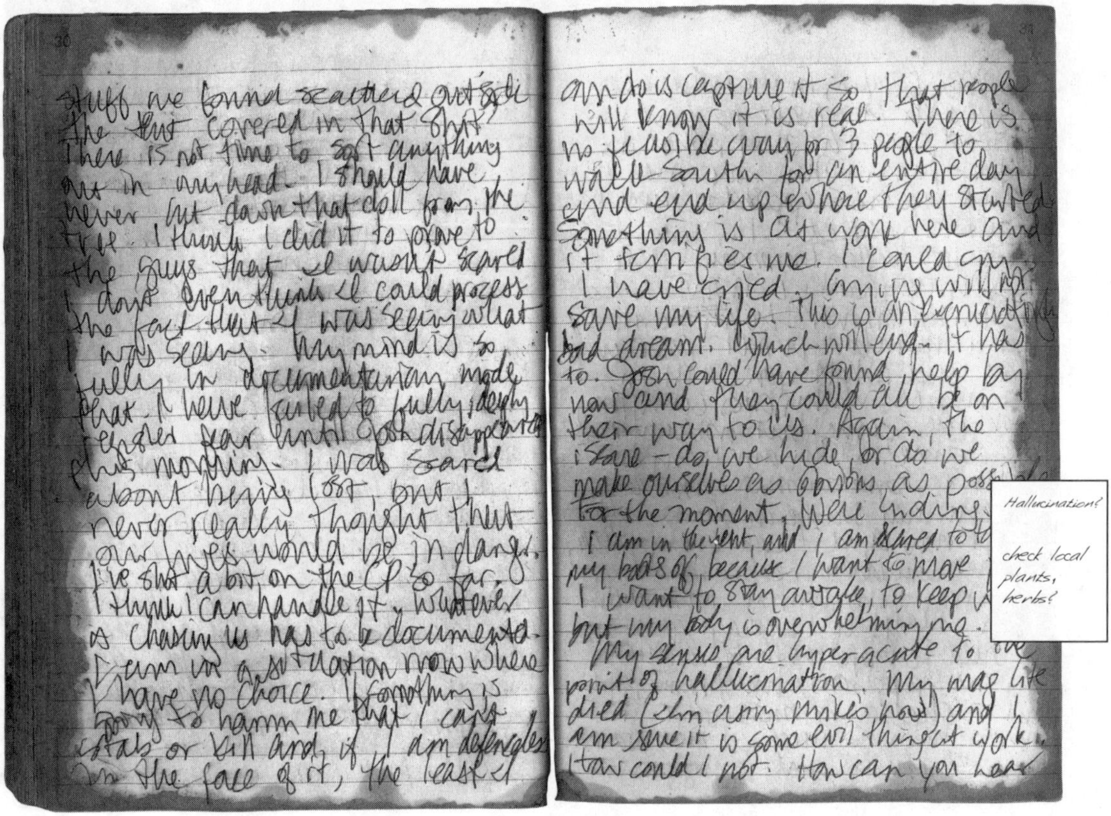

PAGE 30

. . . stuff we found scattered outside the tent covered in that shit. There is not time to sort anything out in my head. I should have never cut down that doll from the tree. I think I did it to prove to the guys that I wasn't scared. I don't even think I could process the fact that I was seeing what I was seeing. My mind is so fully in documentation mode that I have failed to fully, deeply register fear until Josh disappeared this morning. I was scared about being lost, but I never really thought that our lives would be in danger. I've shot a bit on the CP so far. I think I can handle it. Whatever is chasing us has to be documented. I am in a situation now where I have no choice. If something is going to harm me that I can't stab or kill and if I am defenseless in the face of it, the least I . . .

PAGE 31

. . . can do is capture it so that people will know it is real. There is no feasible way for 3 people to walk south for an entire day and end up where they started. Something is at work here and it terrifies me. I could cry. I have cried. Crying will not save my life. This is an excruciatingly bad dream. Which will end. It has to. Josh could have found help by now and they could all be on their way to us. Again, the issue—do we hide, or do we make ourselves as obvious as possible. For the moment, we're hiding. I am in the tent, and I am scared to take my boots off because I want to move fast. I want to stay awake to keep watch, but my body is overwhelming me. My senses are hyperacute to the point of hallucination. My mag lite died (I'm using Mike's now) and I am sure it is some evil thing at work. How could I not. How can you hear . . .

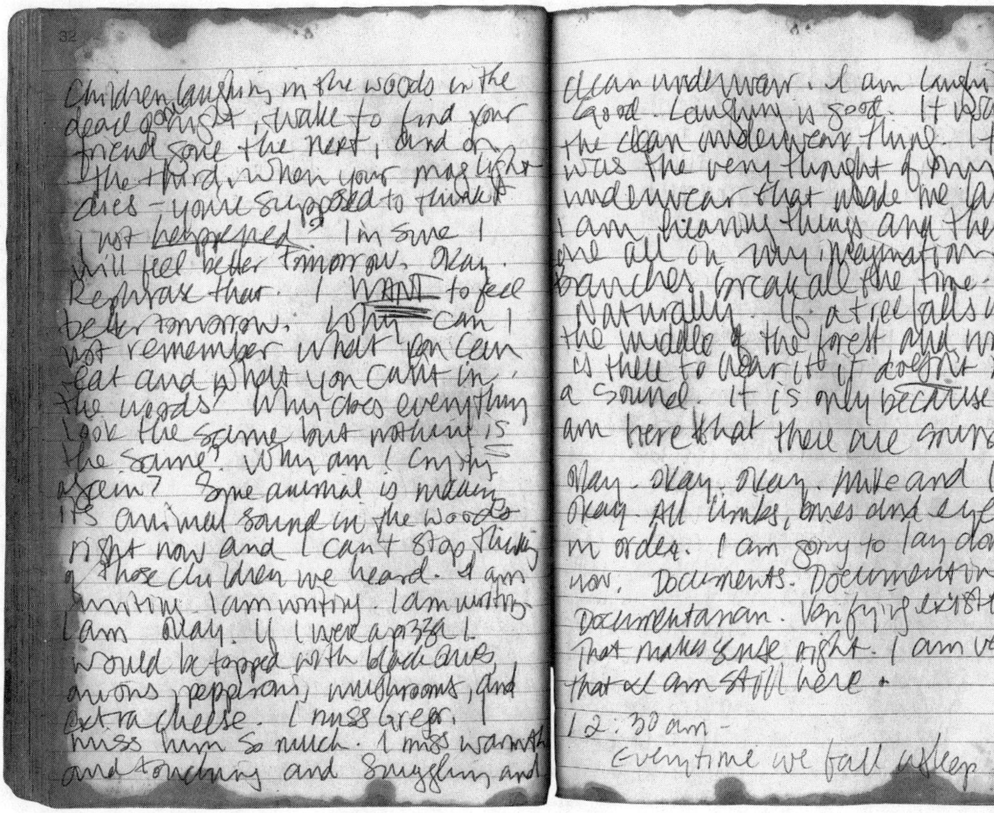

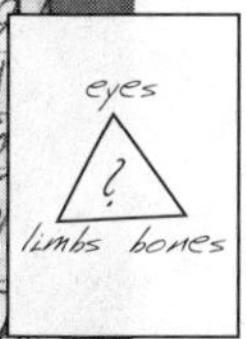

PAGE 32

. . . children laughing in the woods in the dead of one night, wake to find your friend gone the next, and on the third, when your mag light dies—you're supposed to think [it's] not happened? I'm sure I will feel better tomorrow. Okay, rephrase that. I WANT to feel better tomorrow. Why can I not remember what you can eat and what you can't in the woods? Why does everything look the same but nothing is the same? Why am I crying again? Some animal is making it's animal sound in the woods right now and I can't stop thinking of those children we heard. I am writing. I am writing. I am writing. I am okay. If I were a pizza I would be topped with black olives, onions, pepperoni, mushrooms, and extra cheese. I miss Gregg. I miss him so much. I miss warmth and touching and snuggling and . . .

PAGE 33

. . . clean underwear. I am laughing now. Good. Laughing is good. It was the clean underwear thing. It was the very thought of my underwear that made me laugh. I am hearing things and they are all in my imagination. Branches break all the time. Naturally. If a tree falls in the middle of the forest and no one is there to hear it it doesn't make a sound. It is only because I am here that there are sounds.

Okay. Okay. Okay. Mike and I are okay. All limbs, bones and eyes in order. I am going to lay down now. Documents. Documenting. Documentation. Verifying existence. That makes sense right. I am verifying that I am still here.

12:30 am—

Everytime we fall asleep is . . .

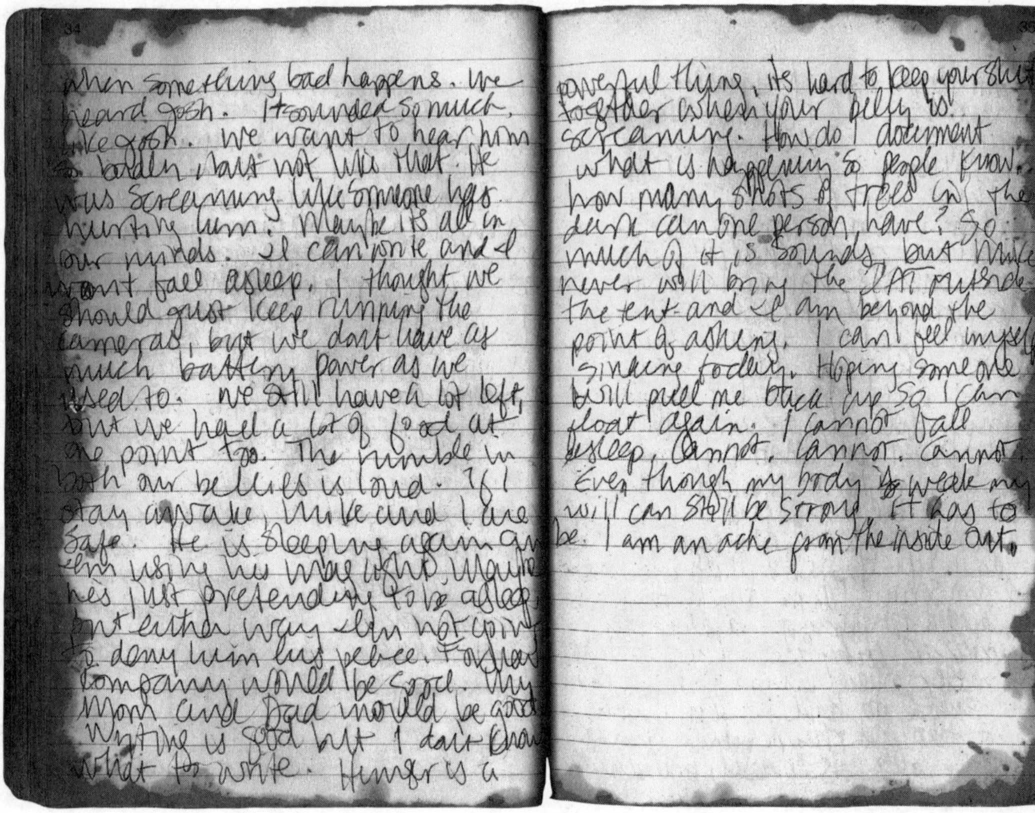

PAGE 34

. . . when something bad happens. We heard Josh. It sounded so much like Josh. We want to hear him so badly, but not like that. He was screaming like someone was hurting him. Maybe it's all in our minds. I can write and I won't fall asleep. I thought we should just keep running the cameras, but we don't have as much battery power as we used to. We still have a lot left, but we had a lot of food at one point, too. The rumble in both our bellies is loud. If I stay awake, Mike and I are safe. He is sleeping again and I'm using his mag light. Maybe he's just pretending to be asleep, but either way I'm not going to deny him his peace. For now company would be good. My mom and dad would be good. Writing is good, but I don't know what to write. Hunger is a . . .

PAGE 35

. . . powerful thing. It's hard to keep your shit together when your belly is screaming. How do I document what is happening so people know. How many shots of trees in the dark can one person have? So much of it is sounds, but Mike never will bring the DAT outside the tent and I am beyond the point of asking. I can feel myself sinking today. Hoping someone will pull me back up so I can float again. I cannot fall asleep. Cannot. Cannot. Cannot. Even though my body is weak my will can still be strong. It has to be. I am an ache from the inside out.

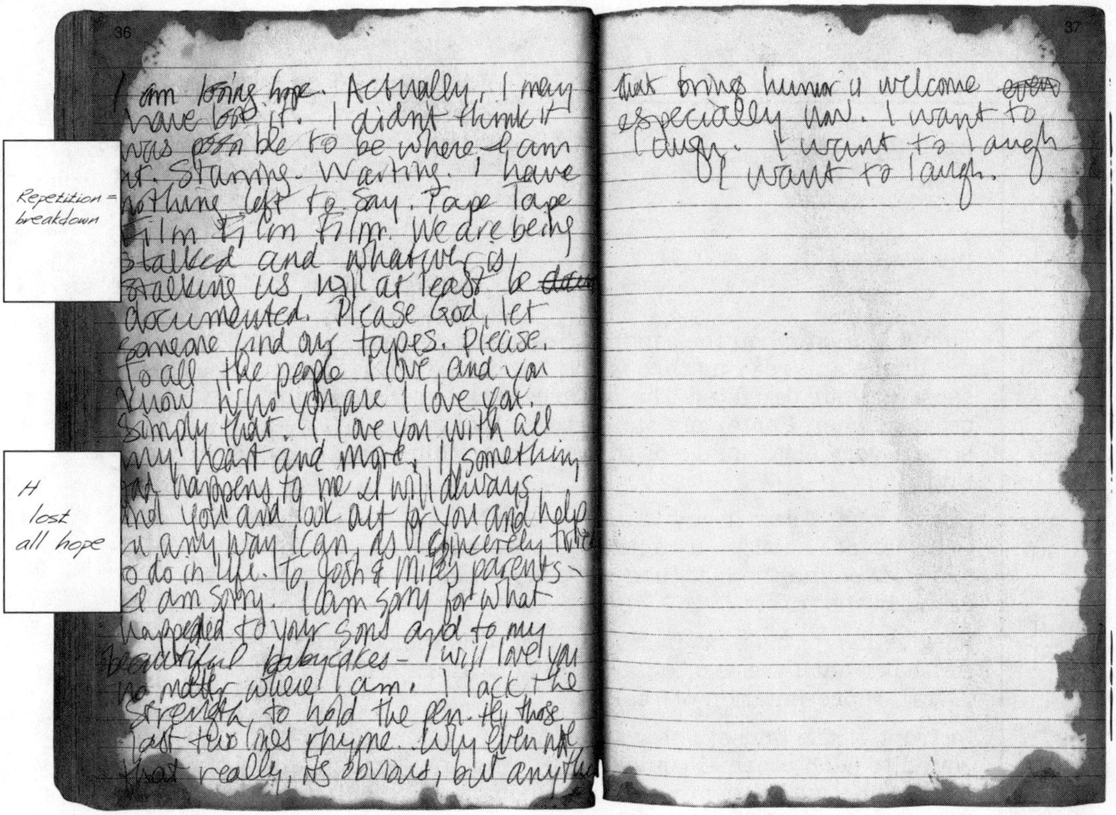

PAGE 36

I am losing hope. Actually, I may have lost it. I didn't think it was possible to be where I am at. Staring. Waiting I have nothing left to say. Tape Tape Film Film Film. We are being stalked and whatever is stalking us will at least be documented. Please God, let someone find our tapes. Please. To all the people I love, and you know who you are I love you. Simply that. I love you with all my heart and more. If something bad happens to me I will always find you and look out for you and help in anyway I can as I sincerely tried to do in my life. To Josh & Mike's parents—I am sorry. I am sorry for what happened to your sons and to my beautiful babycakes—I will love no matter where I am. I lack the strength to hold the pen. Hey, those last two lines rhyme. Why even [noe] that really, its obvious, but anything . . .

PAGE 37

. . . that brings humor is welcome especially now. I want to laugh. I want to laugh. I want to laugh.

April 25, 1996

Dear Angela:

Thank you so much for sending Heather's journal. Holding it in my hands and reading through it, I received a very strong sense of your daughter. The pictures you sent helped, too, because when I enter my state—as I did last night—I need to have a very clear image of the person or thing I'm trying to find.

Here's what I saw in my trance. I didn't see Heather—but I did see a house. I believe it to be the house you described to me over the phone the last time we talked—the house that Heather found in the forest.

Forgive me if this next part sounds a little melodramatic—realize that what I see is often a metaphorical, rather than a literal, representation of reality.

In front of the house, I saw three men lying on the ground, bound to each other—I couldn't quite see how—in the shape of a triangle. One of them was Buck Buchanan. I didn't recognize the other two. I felt an awful sense of apprehension witnessing this scene, as if something terrible were about to happen.

I'm certain this relates somehow to your daughter's disappearance. I need to know a lot more about the case to help you, though. So I'm cutting short my trip here, and will be flying back into Washington on the night of the 27th. I'll call you from the airport.

Sincerely,

Diane Ahlquist

TO: RESEARCHSEARCH@[redacted]

FROM: BUCK001@[redacted]

DATE: 4-25-96

You were right.

I spoke to Cravens. The house where the footage was found—it was Parr's.

I want to see that area, search through it completely, and I want you and Whately there with me. I had him clear his schedule, and I want you to clear yours. Early next week.

—Buck

P.S.—Get all that Blair Witch nonsense out of your head, because we are going to spend a week in that forest if we have to.

THE BLACK HILLS

A partial timeline of the events of late April 1996. Hours and minutes are approximate.

APRIL 27TH 5:10 P.M.	Diane Ahlquist lands at Washington, D.C.'s Dulles International Airport. After phoning Angela Donahue, she rents a car and drives to the Donahue home, arriving at 9:15 p.m.
APRIL 28TH 10:00 A.M.	Diane Ahlquist and Buck Buchanan speak by telephone.
APRIL 28TH 11:00 A.M.	Diane Ahlquist and Angela Donahue drive into Burkittsville, seeking Mary Brown. They fail to find her.
APRIL 29TH 10:00 A.M.	Buck Buchanan, Stephen Whately, and Carlos Sonenberg rendezvous at BPIA headquarters. The three men drive to the Donahue household, where they hold a briefing with Diane Ahlquist and Angela and John Donahue.
APRIL 30TH 8:30 A.M.	The four investigators drive into Burkittsville, where they finally find and speak with Mary Brown.
APRIL 30TH 10:00 A.M.	The investigators, along with Diane Ahlquist, hike into the Black Hills Forest. At Diane Ahlquist's insistence, the party duplicates as closely as possible the route taken by Heather, Josh, and Mike.
APRIL 30TH 2:00 P.M.	The party reaches the archaeological site where the footage was found, and begin searching.
APRIL 30TH 7:30 P.M.	Darkness falls. The search is halted.
APRIL 30TH 9:30 P.M.	Diane Ahlquist prepares the Ritual Circle.
APRIL 30TH 12:00 A.M.	The Wiccan Sabbat of Beltane.

Evening of April 28th—At the Donahues, Diane Ahlquist uses her laptop to leave Buck Buchanan the following note.

Buck:

I'm sorry if I seemed a little harsh at dinner. I wanted to make sure I got my point across—Heather knew what she was getting into. What I didn't want to say with Angela and John there is that she took some foolish chances. I want to make sure we don't.

Tomorrow at midnight marks the observance of the ritual Sabbat of Beltane—the season of renewal, of new life. I don't think the timing is a coincidence: I don't believe in coincidences. There's a reason why we're going to be there in the forest, on this particular date.

That reason is that I am destined to make contact with Heather Donahue. To do so, I'll need the help of you and your associates. I ask that you simply obey my instructions before, during, and after the ceremony.

I know you don't believe in any of this, Buck. But please, please humor me: this forest is an evil place. I can sense that already. I told you what I saw after reading Heather's journal. And after spending this weekend going over the material you gave to Angela on the Blair Witch legend, I don't mind telling you that I'm extremely frightened. The danger there will be great. I can protect us, if you'll let me.

I'll see you bright and early.

—Diane

Same evening. Carlos Sonenberg leaves the following message on the BPIA answering machine.

BUCHANAN'S
PRIVATE INVESTIGATIVE AGENCY, INC.
Serving Since 1940

This Report Constitutes Confidential Work Product and May Further Constitute Work Product of the Nature of an Attorney-Client Privilege

April 28, 1996
Re: BPIA #94-117

CS: Jennifer, this is Carlos. It's about 8:30 p.m. on Sunday night the 28th. Tomorrow morning, first thing, call me here at the Donahues'. I need a copy of the original search party's map of this area, and a transcript of the interview Buck had with Mary Brown. That psychic who's here had a dream about her last night, how she was trying to warn us about something. I don't mind telling you this stuff is weirding me out a little bit. I'm going to be glad to get back to pawing through trash. Talk to you later.

Professional Services Center • 2130 Topanga Creek Boulevard • Cummington, VA • 22769-8990
Office: (927) [redacted] • Local Pager: (927) [redacted]

BUCHANAN'S
PRIVATE INVESTIGATIVE AGENCY, INC.
Serving Since 1940

This Report Constitutes Confidential Work Product and May Further Constitute Work Product of the Nature of an Attorney-Client Privilege

April 30, 1996
Re: BPIA #94-117
Transcript of Tape 94-117-146

Carlos Sonenberg: So it's all right if we record this?

Mary Brown: Yes.

Diane Ahquist: All right, Mary. Let's start over again. We were talking about the dream I had last night.

MB: That's why you came down here to see me.

DA: That's right. Because in my dream, you were trying to warn me about something. You said I had to be careful about going into the forest because—

MB: Because of the witch. Just like I told that other girl. The one making the film.

CS: Heather Donahue?

MB: Heather, yes. You need to be careful, too.

CS: Me?

MB: Yes, hold on a minute. I'll be right back.

[sound of door shutting]

CS: She's a piece of work.

DA: She's all right. Be nice.

CS: I am. We're supposed to meet Buck in a half an hour.

DA: This won't take long. Here she is.

MB: This candle is for you.

CS: Thanks. But why do I need this?

MB: She knows.

DA: I do. Can I ask you something else, Mary? Before, you told Buck that you'd seen Joshua Leonard after they went missing. You haven't seen anything else unusual like that recently, have you?

MB: No.

Professional Services Center • 2130 Topanga Creek Boulevard • Cummington, VA • 22769-8990
Office: (927) • Local Pager: (927)

Transcript of a phone conversation between Jen Colton and Buck Buchanan conducted 6:20 PM EST 30 April 1996. The storm Buchanan refers to made communication later that evening impossible.

BUCHANAN'S
PRIVATE INVESTIGATIVE AGENCY, INC.
Serving Since 1940

This Report Constitutes Confidential Work Product and May Further Constitute Work Product of the Nature of an Attorney-Client Privilege

April 30, 1996
Re: BPIA #94-117
Transcript of Tape 94-117-147

Jen Colton: Hello?

Buck Buchanan: It's Buck. What's going on?

JC: I'm about to head out to talk to Mrs. Wilbraham.

CDB: You went over the ground rules with her husband?

JC: I sure did. It's all set. What's going on up there?

CDB: Not a lot. We're at the site, and we've been searching the entire afternoon. We're about to call it quits—looks like it might rain.

JC: Not a cloud in the sky down here.

CDB: Yeah, I don't know where this came from. It was supposed to be clear all night. We're not really equipped for a storm.

JC: Should I come up there? I could bring rain gear.

CDB: No, that's not necessary. But do me a favor. Take the—[unintelligible]

JC: Say again. You're breaking up.

CDB: Must be the storm. Take the cellular with you—[unintelligible] I'll check in later tonight.

JC: All right.

CDB: Talk to you later. Good-bye.

JC: Bye.

Professional Services Center • 2130 Topanga Creek Boulevard • Cummington, VA • 22769-8990
Office: (927) [redacted] • Local Pager: (927) [redacted]

The following transcript details the events that took place roughly between 9:30 and shortly after midnight on the evening of April 30th, 1996. What you see here has been substantially edited: the entire transcript runs close to two hundred pages long.

BUCHANAN'S

PRIVATE INVESTIGATIVE AGENCY, INC.

Serving Since 1940

This Report Constitutes Confidential Work Product and May Further Constitute Work Product of the Nature of an Attorney-Client Privilege

April 30, 1996

Re: BPIA #94-117

Transcript of Tape 94-117-01

[EDITED—9:44 P.M. EST]

Diane Ahlquist: In the Wiccan tradition, black candles are used to banish the presence of evil.

Carlos Sonenberg: What about the knife?

DA: That's if you get out of line.

CS: Very funny.

DA: It's really for me to help prepare the candles—I'll carve some symbols into them. Like this.

Stephen Whately: What do those symbols mean?

DA: You wouldn't believe me if I told you.

[EDITED—9:47 P.M. EST]

DA: Is that microphone going to pick all this up?

SW: You can walk a hundred feet away and whisper—it'll hear you.

DA: Good. Then I think we're ready.

Buck Buchanan: All right.

DA: Will you get the candles, Stephen? And Carlos, if you could place the crystals—there, and there. Good. Now let's all face toward the north, please—away from the rocks behind us.

SW: Shit. It's starting to rain again.

[EDITED—10:14 P.M. EST]

DA: I summon the circle, the circle I summon!
A place of protection for all who would come in
The world between worlds here now given birth
Through blessings on fire, air, water and earth
Now we enter the circle—here, through this break in the line.
Walk around the circle clockwise, and sit. Good.

CS: Do we have to join hands?

DA: If you like. It's not necessary.

CDB: What happens now?

DA: You really want to know?

CDB: I do.

DA: Within the circle, we've now created sacred space. A space where we can move between dimensions—this physical one, and the one beyond. As this is Beltane—a time of transition—the walls between the dimensions are particularly easy to breach.

[EDITED—10:41 P.M. EST]

SW: What are we supposed to do while she's in this trance state?

CS: I think we're supposed to be quiet.

SW: Forgive me for breathing, but I'm fucking soaked and freezing. I'm going to get a jacket.

CDB: Stay in the circle.

SW: All right, all right. Ignore my screams when my balls fall off.

CS: Did you hear something?

SW: No.

CDB: No.

CS: It sounded like a girl, crying.

[EDITED—11:10 P.M. EST]

CS: There's that sound again.

SW: I think I heard it too.

CDB: Go check it out, Steve.

CS: I thought we were supposed to stay in the circle.

CDB: I'm using my discretion. You have your gun?

SW: Right here.

CDB: Be careful.

[EDITED—11:12 P.M. EST]

CBD: What's the matter?

SW: I fell—twisted my ankle.

CDB: I'll go.

CS: No, I'll go.

CDB: You sure about that?

CS: Of course I'm sure.

CDB: All right. Don't take any chances.

CS: I won't. I'll be right back.

DA: [unintelligible]

SW: How long has she been babbling like that?

CDB: Started right after you left.

SW: What's she saying?

CDB: How would I know? Does that even sound like English to you?

[EDITED—11:19 P.M. EST]

SW: Shit. Do you want me to go after him?

CDB: Give him a few more minutes.

DA: I'm in the house.

SW: What did she just say?

CDB: She's in the house?

SW: What the fuck does that mean?

CDB: Take it easy, Steve.

SW: Diane?

CDB: Look at her eyes. She can't hear you.

DA: Oh, God, it's everywhere! I can sense it everywhere!

SW: That doesn't even sound like her.

DA: I'm running through the house. Up the stairs. Down the stairs. Mike? Mike, where are you?

SW: This is creeping me out. Buck?

DA: I'm in the basement. Oh, God! The smell!

CDB: I don't like this at all. Let's wake her up.

SW: I'm with you. Let's snap her out of it, let's find Sonenberg, and let's get the hell out of here.

DA: Mike? Mike, what's the matter? Why are you standing like that?

SW: Jesus, what was that? Was that Sonenberg?

CDB: Go! Go get him!

SW: [unintelligible]

DA: MIKE!

Professional Services Center • 2130 Topanga Creek Boulevard • Cummington, VA • 22769-8990
Office: (927) ███ • Local Pager: (927) ███

Transcript of a phone call placed 1:10 a.m., Wednesday, May 1, 1996

BUCHANAN'S
PRIVATE INVESTIGATIVE AGENCY, INC.
Serving Since 1940

This Report Constitutes Confidential Work Product and May Further Constitute Work Product of the Nature of an Attorney-Client Privilege

May 1, 1996
Re: BPIA #94-117
[1:10 A.M. EST]

Operator: This is 911. Can I have your name and the location you're calling from?

CDB: This is Buck Buchanan, and I'm calling you from Black Rock Road just outside Burkittsville, Maryland. I'd say we're about fifteen minutes due west off Route 67.

Operator: You're on a cellular phone?

CDB: I am.

Operator: What's the matter, sir?

CDB: We have two injuries. A male, age twenty-seven, with a broken arm. A female, same approximate age, in some sort of a trance—I can't snap her out of it.

Operator: Do you need instructions from medical personnel?

CDB: I'd like to talk to a doctor if you've got one handy.

Operator: Hold the line, sir, and I'll see if I can patch one through from the hospital. We're dispatching an ambulance right now.

CDB: Thank you, operator.

Professional Services Center • 2130 Topanga Creek Boulevard • Cummington, VA • 22769-8990
Office: (927) [redacted] • Local Pager: (927) [redacted]

THE AFTERMATH

May 11, 1996

Angela Donahue

Dear Angela:

Thank you so much for your note, and the flowers that you sent while I was in the hospital. They really brightened up the room.

I wish I could remember more about what happened to me the other night: I wish I could give you any definitive sense of what might have happened to Heather. In my trance, I recall seeing images—a fallen log bridging a river, a house standing at the top of a hill—and I recall seeing Heather, walking through the woods with Joshua and Michael. And then at some point, I was Heather: it was as if I was standing in her shoes, experiencing everything she wrote about in the journal.

Nothing like that has ever happened to me before. I wish I could remember more of it. I'm glad Buck convinced me to let him tape-record that evening: when I get out of here in a few days, I'm going to listen to that tape and see if it sparks any memories.

Perhaps if those memories come back, I'll be able to remember more specific things about Heather as well. Usually, when I go into a trance, I pick up images of where the object or person I'm looking for is in the here and now. Hopefully, those memories will come back to me as well.

Best to you and Jim,

Diane

Angela Donahue sent this letter to Buck Buchanan after he had called to tell her he was dropping the case.

May 30, 1996

Buck Buchanan
2130 Topanga Creek Boulevard
Cunnington, Va 22769

Dear Buck:

You shouldn't for a second feel guilty. You told us there might come a time when you didn't think your work on the case would be productive, and we've reached it, and so that's all there is to it. Jim and I are going to continue to press foward with the search. We're meeting an investigator from New York — one of Jim's colleagues works with him quite a lot.

If you don't mind, I may call you from time to time with some questions. The other investigator - his name is McKeown - may do the same.

After spending so much time with you, Jim and I consider you as much our friend as someone who worked for us. You (and any of your people) will always be welcome here. And be sure and pass along my thanks to all of them for their hard work.

All the best,

Angela Donahue

TO: JCOLTON7

FROM: RESEARCH

DATE: August 4, 1996

RE: THE GRAND CANYON

This sure is a big hole.

Stayed at a hotel called El Tovar right at the Canyon's edge last night, and woke up early to see the sunrise. Spectacular view—it sounds clichéd, but when you look at something like this, you really are reminded of your relative place in the grand scheme of things.

And while I was sitting there, gazing at the majesty of the unspoiled wilderness, a deer came along and stole my croissant. They're so used to tourists coming here that they have absolutely no fear of people. Things like that used to make me furious—how we're turning the whole world into a collection of little theme parks. De-fanging nature, as it were.

After what happened in the forest, I really don't mind it as much. I like feeling safe. And I'm glad to be away from everything that could remind me of the case—taking some time to travel was absolutely the right thing to do, and I thank you again for suggesting the idea.

I expect to be back in Washington on Labor Day, and I'll see you then. You take care—and give my best to Buck, and Whately.

—CS

BUCHANAN'S
PRIVATE INVESTIGATIVE AGENCY, INC.
Serving Since 1940

This Report Constitutes Confidential Work Product and May Further Constitute Work Product of the Nature of an Attorney-Client Privilege

June 4, 1996
Re: BPIA #94-117

CASE SUMMARY
TO: FILE
FROM: BUCK BUCHANAN

On October 21, 1994, Heather Donahue, Joshua Leonard, and Michael Williams disappeared in the Black Hills Forest near Burkittsville, Maryland. Despite intensive investigation by law enforcement authorities and this agency, their fate remains a mystery.

In the opinion of this investigator, that status is unlikely to change.

There are many unexplainable and conflicting elements to this case that have the appearance of clues, yet when fully explored turn out to be dead ends. Though I am convinced of the absolute integrity of (in particular) Heather Donahue, the possibility still exists that this is all a massive hoax perpetrated by the students themselves.

This memo will serve as a cover letter when copies of this agency's efforts are forwarded to other investigators who may be assigned to the case.

I will be available for consultation at the numbers listed below.

Professional Services Center • 2130 Topanga Creek Boulevard • Cummington, VA • 22769-8990
Office: (927) ████ • Local Pager: (927) ████

BUCHANAN'S
PRIVATE INVESTIGATIVE AGENCY, INC.

Serving Since 1940

This Report Constitutes Confidential Work Product and May Further Constitute Work Product of the Nature of an Attorney-Client Privilege

May 26, 1999

D. A. Stern

Dear Mr. Stern:

I've gone over the pages you sent me, and everything looks fine. You have my approval to proceed with publication.

It seems hard to believe it's been three years since I worked on this case: looking over this material, it all came back to me pretty quickly. It was a unique set of circumstances we faced in this investigation, and I'm proud of the work we did under those conditions. I wish we'd had more to go on.

As you requested, here's a summary of what the personnel associated with the investigation are doing now. Jenn Colton has gone back to police work: she's a detective with the Miami Police Department. Stephen Whately is still working as a freelance operative: I saw him in Washington last year. Carlos Sonenberg is with the FBI: I believe he's working in their Los Angeles office. Diane Ahlquist still lives in Florida, and as far as I know, continues to work as a psychic.

You know better than I what the filmmakers' families are up to: please say hello to the Donahues for me the next time you talk to them.

Sincerely,

Professional Services Center • 2130 Topanga Creek Boulevard • Cummington, VA • 22769-8990

Office: (927) [redacted] • Local Pager: (927) [redacted]

POSTSCRIPT

In the end, after all the blind alleys, false leads, and maddeningly incomplete accounts of that October weekend when Heather Donahue, Michael Williams, and Joshua Leonard vanished from the face of the earth, we're left with more questions than answers.

Which parts of the Blair Witch legend can be considered historical fact—and which parts must be labeled fiction? Elly Kedward? Eileen Treacle? Rustin Parr? In these pages, I have tried to lay out the key pieces of the mystery surrounding the three students' disappearance, to point out things to you, the reader, that the "experts" missed, things that bear—at the least—further consideration, if not actual re-investigation. Investigation not by the so-called "authorities," either. After all, there are things within this world no lab analysis can explain, dark corners of the world no investigator's flashlight can ever hope to illumine.

It seems to me that all that can be said for certain is that something lives in the Black Hills.

Let whoever goes searching for it beware.

D. A. Stern